Due Benevolence

Due Benevolence:

A Study of Biblical Sexuality
(It May Not Be What You Think!)

Clyde L. Pilkington, Jr.

www.DueBenevolence.com

Due Benevolence: A Study of Biblical Sexuality
by Clyde L. Pilkington, Jr.
Copyright © 2010 by Clyde L. Pilkington, Jr.
All rights reserved.

Original Printing:

Individual articles published in *Due Benevolence,* 2007-2010

Second Printing:

First book edition, 2010

Executive Editor: André Sneidar
Associate Editor: Richard Lemons
Layout and Design: Great Adventure in Faith
Cover design by Clyde L. Pilkington, III

This publication is an attempt to take an honest, fresh look at the subject of sexuality from a Biblical perspective. It is dedicated to the recovery of Biblical truth that has too long remained hidden under the veils of traditionalism, prejudice, misunderstanding, and fear (Mark 7:7, 13).

Readers are encouraged to be as the Bereans and search the Scriptures (Acts 17:10-11; I Thessalonians 5:21). This publication contains mature content and is not intended for minors, nor is it intended to provide personal or legal advice.

ISBN-10:   1-934251-60-7
ISBN-13:   978-1934251-60-7

Published by:

Pilkington & Sons
PO Box 265
Windber, PA 15963

www.DueBenevolence.com

Printed in the United States of America.

CONTENTS

Foreword

SEX: THE DIVINE ORDER OF CREATION

It is not surprising that the mistakes of our [religious] past should have given us a poor view of something that God made and pronounced *"good."* It is almost impossible, now, to divest ourselves of the view that sex is an obscenity.

However strenuously we try to disturb our prejudice against it, the view is deeply ingrained that sex is a power which exercises a hold over life that is at least dangerous and more likely evil. Containment is the common approach, instead of liberation.

Sex is not a monstrous mistake of the Creator, but something for which we may expect that God holds a constructive purpose in view. No doubt that purpose is being served in spite of our upset situation, but how much better if the good for which this faculty was intended could be pinpointed and its drive directed into ways that would benefit all!

Sex is in just about everything. This is not bad, but the natural way of things. Therefore the Christian has to start where the Bible starts, by acknowledging things as God has given them to us. After all, the whole of life is either male or female, and of all the instinctive drives that have been given to us, hunger is the most compelling, but sex is the most pervasive. It naturally touches everything … Indeed life would be cold, hard, and metallic without it. God did not give us a sexless world. It is not for us to fight against God's order of creation, but rather to seek to know more and find the line of purpose to follow.

Kingsley G. Bond
Creative Witness
(Tidings: 1967)

Preface

WHAT IF...?

What if much of what we think we know about sexuality is based upon cultural and religious tradition? Most saints live their lives in bondage to bad doctrine. What if most of us were living our sexual lives in bondage to bad doctrine as well? What if many of those obsessive fears and concerns regarding our sexuality were not true? What if some of those thoughts we have constantly dismissed and oppressed were based upon Godly design, rather than upon sinful passion? What if the so-called "Everyman's Battle" was, in fact, not designed to be a battle, but a precious gift?

I believe that the subject of sexuality is, sadly, one of the most neglected topics of the entire Bible. As a result, the lives of many, if not most, have been adversely affected. Believers wrongfully have been deceived concerning one of God's greatest gifts to man. Marriages have been scarred and damaged.

BE FOREWARNED!

Due Benevolence™ will contain honest, frank discussions about sexuality that will be very biblically graphic, even to the point of what some people would undoubtedly label as inappropriate. Yet the Bible does not pull any punches or beat around the bush with any subject it approaches – and the subject of sexuality is no different. So a word of caution – this publication *will* contain material that could easily be viewed by many as "offensive."

That *Due Benevolence*™ will be controversial may well be a great understatement. The articles will *definitely* go "against the flow." Frankly, you will probably be shocked at what I have to say. In fact, you will probably *not* want to read this book if you do not want your current understanding of sexuality to be challenged.

The purpose of publishing these materials will be basically threefold: (1) to teach as clearly as I can what I understand to be the neglected truths that the Scriptures teach concerning various aspects of sexuality; (2) to guide saints to reclaim their godly gift and enjoyment of sexuality; (3) to help relieve people of undue guilt and bondage produced by the legalistic, moralistic, Victorian religious influence coming from Roman Catholic and Gnostic errors.

If you have a genuine interest in these studies, *"Welcome, brave hearts!"* You will probably not agree with everything you read. Frankly, I do not ask that of you. In fact, I am sure that over the passage of time I, too, will not agree with everything that I have written. I am just "stepping up to the plate" and "taking a swing" at presenting the things I have been studying for the past 30 years. I encourage you to study out what is presented and consider it for yourselves. Take what you can that is valuable and that you find to be the truth of the Scripture. I appreciate the opportunity to share these things with serious seekers.

REGARDING RESOURCES

Over the years I have invested what has been for me a small fortune gathering resource materials for this project. I will be doing my best to give extensive footnotes. It is important for me to provide as much documentation as possible for historical references and other sources. I will be making every honest attempt to share my sources correctly; but since this has been a 30-year quest, I want to apologize beforehand for any oversight in properly acknowledging any resource. I will provide appropriate corrections in future editions if, and as I am made aware of any inadvertent lack of recognition.

A STARTING PLACE

This is not intended to be an exhaustive work. There is much more that could be said on this subject, but this serves only as a sort of starting place. I trust that God will use this to liberate the reader to a fresh study of the Scriptures as they relate to the subject of sexuality. I am convinced that an honest study will reveal that it is not what we think it is.

Along the way I am sure that I will find works written by others along these lines that would make a valuable addition to this work. If so, I will list them on my website devoted to this topic:

www.DueBenevolence.com

Clyde

Clyde L. Pilkington, Jr.

Introduction

An Introduction to Biblical Sexuality

So God created man in His Own image, in the image of God created He him; male and female created He them (Genesis 1:27).

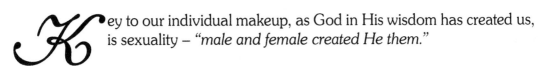

ey to our individual makeup, as God in His wisdom has created us, is sexuality – *"male and female created He them."*

There are many aspects of our lives, but none more characterizing as our sexuality. It has an affect upon every other part. This is no mistake. It is a part of the Divine plan for humanity.

A SCRIPTURAL BACKGROUND

And the LORD God said, It is not good that the man should be alone; I will make him an help meet for him (Genesis 2:18).

After saying "good" seven times in chapter one, we come across the only "not good" of the creation story. Adam was alone – but our wonderful God had a plan!

And the LORD God caused a deep sleep to fall upon Adam, and he slept: and He took one of his ribs, and closed up the flesh instead thereof; and the rib, which the LORD God had taken from man, made He a woman, and brought her unto the man. And Adam said, "This is now bone of my bones, and flesh of my flesh: she shall be called Woman, because she was taken out of Man." Therefore shall a man leave his father and his mother, and shall cleave unto his wife: and they shall be one flesh. And they were both naked, the man and his wife, and were not ashamed (Genesis 2:21-25).

Ever since the garden, one of the things that preoccupies the heart of the male is the female. There are many beauties of the handiwork of God: trees, flowers, mountains, beaches, sunsets … but none match the beauty of the female![1]

A PERSONAL BACKGROUND

I have always been in love with females – my mother, my sister, my wife, my daughter. I always preferred to play with the girls when I was little, and as I grew up. I was always in awe of them – their tenderness, sweetness, and beauty! I have never lost that awe. I believe that the woman is the crowning work of God's creative beauty!

I came from a very loving family. I have a wonderful heritage of marital love, but my family is probably just like many of yours – we just never discussed sexual issues, because they were things that you simply didn't talk about. That was just the religious and cultural side of the society in which I was raised. By no means do I fault my parents for this; that is the way that they were brought up, and the way that their parents were brought up, too.

As for "the Church," it was not any better in providing help in these areas. The only preaching that I ever remember hearing on sexual issues was negative. There were never any sermons or Bible studies on the positive aspects of sexuality.

Many passages began to capture my heart and thinking as a young married man – Scriptures that I never heard expounded. From the very beginning of marital life, I determined to dedicate my life to being the kind of husband that God wanted me to be, which I believed from my study of the Scripture clearly included love making.

As a result, I read every Christian marriage book that I could find. They usually proved to be of some help, but never provided me the training and frankness that I so very much needed and desired. There is a simple reason for this.

---

1. DOING GOD'S WORK: "God has given them [the females] beauty. It would be an insult to God's creation to hide the beauty that God wants everyone to see. Think of it as doing God's work." – Gene Simmons, *The Apprentice*, 2008.
   APPRECIATION OF FEMALE BEAUTY: "I look at the picture of Rachael Ray, and I thank God for Rachael Ray because I think Rachael Ray is really cute." – Martin Zender, *Clanging Gong News*, 2009, Vol. 1, No. 3.

RELIGION'S NEGATIVE
APPROACH TO SEXUALITY

Christendom has been under great bondage in most areas, including sexually. There is clear and abundant history of negativity toward sexual topics. Origen – Augustine – Roman Catholicism – Puritanism – Victorianism – have all played their role in this bondage. Historically we can trace this body-negative theology to the Gnostics.

Sadly, many, if not most marital relationships have been crippled by religion! The moralist's system has abused the husband-wife relationship in so many ways!

Early in my ministry I knew a couple who grew up "in the church." After they had been married for about a year, the husband confided in me that they had never had sex. His wife viewed nudity and sex as dirty. This was an eye-opener for me. Something was desperately wrong with our "Christian morality!"

Although I have actively studied sexuality since I was first married, the first years were not very productive, as I had an extremely legalistic mindset. This began changing in 1985 as I started learning more about grace, and the progressive revelation of Scripture. Drastic changes occurred in my understanding and life. I was greatly liberated. This liberation allowed me to seek clearer marital information. This time I was able to acquire information outside of Christendom. How appropriate was Christ's statement, *"For the children of this world are in their generation wiser than the children of light"* (Luke 16:8)!

Since that time I have continued my studies of the Bible and any other materials that I have found to help me be a better husband, and to enrich my marriage. I have learned how women can become multi-orgasmic, to the point of *female* ejaculation. This is something that I always *knew* was possible from my study of Proverbs chapter 5:15-19.

> Drink **waters** out of your own **cistern,** and **running waters** out of your own **well.** Let your **fountains** be dispersed abroad, and **rivers of waters** in the streets ... Let your **fountain** be blessed: and rejoice with the wife of your youth. Let her be as the loving hind and pleasant roe; let her breasts satisfy you at all times; and be ravished always with her love.

As we can see from this passage, the wife is spoken of as a cistern, well and fountain. She is a source of water[2] – water that is to be enjoyed! Don't mistake the significance of this understanding. These are things that can allow husbands and wives to enjoy married life in a far greater fullness! (Husbands, imagine spending years in a marriage without orgasm or ejaculation, and yet this is what many wives have had to endure.)

It is my belief that husbands and wives should live in love. I believe that, ideally, they should spend the majority of every day together. They are to enjoy a continual state of love making – life spent in foreplay. Even work should be a marriage haven – playful and frisky – "sneaking" kisses – little quick rendezvous. They should enjoy the richness of marital bliss together.

SEXUALITY: ONE OF THE HIGHEST EXPRESSIONS OF LOVE

Sexuality, by divine design, represents one of the highest expressions of human love. In addition to expressing our love for another, sexuality increases the *bonds* in marriage, for the ultimate sexual act of intercourse is a powerfully uniting *bond* that should not be overlooked.

Husbands and wives are able to share a bond that is deeply *physical* and *emotional* – one that is unsurpassed in any other experience. This shared sexual love is extremely pleasurable, but is *much more* than that. I believe that this is so by the design of our Creator. He has purposefully made us *very* sexual creatures!

Sexual acts help keep our hearts bound to our wives. They help keep the extremes of our masculinity in balance. As we experience intimate sexual exchanges, our hearts are kept much more tender and gentle toward our wives, and towards others as well. This is a result of the feminine balance of masculinity that can be observed foremost in sexual acts. I presume that this is a natural product of intimate, loving sexuality as designed by God.

Thus, the power of sexual expression! What greater expression of tenderness, and emotional and physical love can we have than the power of sexual expression? What a wonderful testimony sexuality is to shared marital love! Oh, the joy of sharing such a precious bond with one that you love!

---

2. This is the reason for using a picture of a well on this book's title page.

LOVE AND SEXUALITY

One author writes:

> The most important love expression of mankind is sexuality ... The end and aim of the sex act is ... the expression of love! ... It is sexuality that provides us with a human outlet and human expression of divine love.

> Active and vigorous sex lives, unimpeded by inhibition and witch's tales, express the fullness of love ... Sexual excesses are the product of the absence of love ... Satisfactory sexual experience is the result of love, and never the cause of it.

> Your sex life expresses always your own understanding of love. But love never proceeds into the understanding solely through the relationship of a man and his mate. The understanding of true love comes only from the relationship of man with God. No human being can truly love another unless he first knows the love of God. A man who loves God loves life; and his marriage will be a perfect fusion of his understanding of love.

> God is love, and there is nothing sinful and shameful about God. Sex is life expressing love. No one will deny that sexual intercourse can give pleasure. What unholy masochism prompts us ever to believe that such pleasure is sinful and wrong? We didn't make our bodies and couldn't if we tried. Do we presume to state that the great Creator made a mistake by accompanying sex relations with pleasurable sensations? It is just as sensible for us to say that it is sinful for eyes to see, and to set about forming organizations for the putting out of people's eyes.[3]

Oh, the prophets of evil and shame and fear and hate have made their inroads when they have woven into our thinking the hideous tendency to believe that everything painful is good and everything pleasurable is evil. We have martyred ourselves too long.

THE BASIS OF FAITH AND GRACE

As we begin to study these issues together, it is extremely important that we remember that the bottom line of our sexual lives (as well as *all* other areas of our lives) is faith and grace! These are the foundational principles set forth in Romans chapter 14.

---

3. Uell Andersen (1917-1986), *Three Magic Words* (1972), pp. 232-239.

Faith

There is the principle of personal faith. Our walk before the Lord is to be one based upon faith! This faith is to be *personal,* and without the dominion of men.

Whatsoever is not of faith is sin (Romans 14:23).

Let every man be fully persuaded in his own mind (Romans 14:5).

Do you have faith? have it to yourself before God (Romans 14:22).

Not for that we have dominion over your faith, but are helpers of your joy: for by faith you stand (II Corinthians 1:24).

Our lifestyle is to be one borne out of *personal* faith!

Grace

Then there is the principle of divine grace. God does not want us to judge each other regarding our *personal* faith. This is a real test of grace in our lives. It is easy to love and accept those who mirror our beliefs and practices – that takes little if any grace; but to love and accept a brother who has differing beliefs and practices requires a work of God's grace in our hearts. What it really takes is the willingness to give up our assumed dominion over the lives of others.

Wherefore receive one another, as Christ also received us to the glory of God (Romans 15:7).

Who are you who judges another man's servant? to his own master he stands or falls. Yea, he shall be held up: for God is able to make him stand (Romans 14:4).

But why do you judge your brother? or why do you set at nought your brother? for we shall all stand before the judgment seat of Christ (Romans 14:10).

God has called us to a life of grace, not law – a life that proceeds from the heart of love, not from externals.

Do we by grace afford others the liberty to study the Bible for themselves? Do we permit them to come to their own position of *personal* faith before God? Do we allow them to walk in accordance with that faith to His glory as an act of worship? Do we let them live their lives heartily, as unto the Lord, and not unto men?

THE WORK THAT FOLLOWS

The work that follows is a continuing study. I have been working on this material for many years, but much more work is still needed. As I present the material, it will have many gaps and much lack of flow. I will be sharing portions of my studies that are sufficiently ready to be of any practical use. It literally represents THOUSANDS of hours of personal study on this subject. I *do not* say this to point to the correctness of my positions. I do so to show the importance that this subject has with me!

I have for many years desired to teach upon this subject. Over the past few years I have been given the courage of heart to talk to others about the things that I have learned. My goal is to help liberate the saints from the bondage and fear of religion, and share with you the glorious things that I have learned from Scripture.

I invite you to enjoy **Due Benevolence**™, if you can!

Chapter 1

Our Bodies

On the outset of our studies on sexuality, it would be immensely profitable to acquire a divine understanding concerning our bodies. It is extremely sad just how many dear saints battle endlessly simply to survive the "Christian life." At the center of this conflict is a great misunderstanding of the very nature of our bodies. There is a deep-rooted body-negative view. Multitudes labor under the bondage of such a perverted view. Simply put, many are miserable with themselves. They often find themselves at their wit's end. Their hearts and souls desperately ache for real and lasting relief. Just where is the life of joy and victory that they hear so much about?

There are some basic truths related to the body that are crucial for us to see and embrace. Without a grasp of these simple, precious truths, we are left for prey to the dreadful bondage of religion.

One topic of critical understanding is the word "flesh." The Scriptures convey four basic concepts by the usage of our English word "flesh." These distinct concepts are often confused in our minds to the point of utter frustration and discouragement. Without this being corrected we actually end up struggling against the very core of who God, in His wise and gracious design, has actually made us to be for His Own glory. Let's briefly look at the four ways that our English word "flesh" is used in Scripture.

FLESH: A REFERENCE TO THE BODY
(Godly by divine design)

*But God gives it a body as it has pleased Him, and to every seed his own body. All flesh is not the same flesh: but there is one kind of **flesh of men,** another flesh of beasts, another of fishes, and another of birds* (I Corinthians 15:38-39).

*I am crucified with Christ: nevertheless I live; yet not I, but Christ lives in me: and **the life which I now live in the flesh** I live by the faith of the Son of God, Who loved me, and gave Himself for me* (Galatians 2:20).

*But if I **live in the flesh,** this is the fruit of my labor ... Nevertheless to **abide in the flesh** is more needful for you* (Philippians 1:22, 24).

*And the Word was **made flesh,** and dwelled among us (and we beheld His glory, the glory as of the only Begotten of the Father), full of grace and truth* (John 1:14).

FLESH: A REFERENCE TO MEAT
(Godly by divine design)

*It is good neither to **eat flesh,** nor to drink wine, nor any thing whereby your brother stumbles, or is offended, or is made weak* (Romans 14:21).

*Wherefore, if meat makes my brother to offend, I will **eat no flesh** while the world stands, lest I make my brother to offend* (I Corinthians 8:13).

FLESH: A REFERENCE TO KINSHIP
(Godly by Divine Design)

*Therefore shall a man leave his father and his mother, and shall cleave unto his wife: and they shall be **one flesh*** (Genesis 2:24).

*"Come, and let us sell him to the Ishmeelites, and let not our hand be upon him; for he is our brother and **our flesh."** And his brothers were content* (Genesis 37:27).

*Concerning His Son Jesus Christ our Lord, Who was made of the seed of David according to **the flesh** (Romans 1:3).*

*For I could wish that I myself was accursed from Christ for my brothers, my kinsmen according to **the flesh** ... of whom as concerning **the flesh** Christ came (Romans 9:3, 5).*

FLESH: A REFERENCE TO THE OLD MAN
(Ungodly by the Adamic fall)

*For **when we were in the flesh**, the motions of sins, which were by the law, did work in our members to bring forth fruit unto death ... For I know that in me (that is, **in my flesh,**) [i.e., old identity] (Romans 7:5, 18).*

*So then they who are **in the flesh** cannot please God. **But you are not in the flesh,** but in the Spirit, if so be that the Spirit of God dwells in you. Now if any man has not the Spirit of Christ, he is none of His (Romans 8:8-9).*

*And they who are Christ's **have crucified the flesh** with the affections and lusts (Galatians 5:24).*

The usage of "flesh" in these last three passages is a reference to "the old man" (Romans 6:6; Ephesians 4:22; Colossians 3:9),[1] and as such is a doctrinal term referring to the natural man's identity in fallen Adam. This identity is anchored in his perception of "good and evil:" his giving way to the "evil," or his legalistic efforts to perform the "good."

Yet as we have clearly seen in the example of the earlier passages, this is not the only meaning of "flesh." A destructive teaching arises from our failure to *"rightly divide the Word of Truth"* – to make distinctions based upon the context of each passage. Many misunderstand (or misrepresent!) the word "flesh," used as a reference to our former identity in Adam, and thus apply it to all references to "flesh." The Gnostics mastered this concept, as they taught that all that was related to "the flesh" was "evil." They went on to interpret "the flesh" as anything related

---

1. *"Knowing this, that our old man is crucified with Him, that the body of sin might be destroyed, that henceforth we should not serve sin"* (Romans 6:6).
   "That you put off concerning the former conversation the old man, which is corrupt according to the deceitful lusts" (Ephesians 4:22).
   "Lie not one to another, seeing that you have put off the old man with his deeds" (Colossians 3:9).

to our *physical* body and the physical world around us. This led to horrendous religious abuse which has been present since Paul's day:

> *For you suffer* [allow], *if a man brings you into* **bondage,** *if a man* **devours** *you, if a man* **takes** *of you, if a man* **exalts** *himself, if a man* **smites** *you on the face* (II Corinthians 11:20).

Far from the teaching of the Gnostics, the Scriptures actually teach God's beautiful design of the human body and the physical world.

The Godliness of the Physical Creation

> *it was good* (Genesis 1:4)

> *it was good* (Genesis 1:10)

> *it was good* (Genesis 1:12)

> *it was good* (Genesis 1:18)

> *it was good* (Genesis 1:21)

> *it was good* (Genesis 1:25)

> *And God saw every thing that He had made, and, behold, it was very good* … (Genesis 1:31).

The Wonder of the Physical Creation

> *I will praise You; for I am fearfully and wonderfully made: marvellous are Your works; and that my soul knows right well* (Psalm 139:14).

The Enjoyment of the Physical Creation

> *… God, Who gives us richly all things to enjoy* (I Timothy 6:17).

As we walk in harmony with God, He gives us the grand gift of creation appreciation!

Our Body, God's Temple

*Know you not that your bodies are the members of Christ? … What? know you not that **YOUR body is the temple of the Holy Ghost** which is in you, which you have of God, and you are not your own? For you are bought with a price: **therefore glorify God in YOUR body**, and in your spirit, which are God's* (I Corinthians 6:15, 19-20).

Imagine standing in old Jerusalem, pointing to the Temple and saying, in there *"dwells no good thing."* How absurd! God resided there! It was His dwelling place, and yet, we have the audacity to presume that God's grand dwelling place today – our bodies – is evil? What sad abuse of the truth!

Our Body, God's Holy Acceptable Sacrifice

*I beseech you therefore, brothers, by the mercies of God, that you present **YOUR bodies** a living sacrifice, holy, acceptable unto God, which is your reasonable service* (Romans 12:1).

The Godliness of Self-Love

It is the divine foundation of neighborly love

*You shall love the Lord your God with all your heart, and with all your soul, and with all your strength, and with all your mind; and your neighbor **as yourself*** (Luke 10:27).

*For all the law is fulfilled in one word, even in this; You shall love your neighbor **as yourself*** (Galatians 5:14).

It is the divine foundation of marital love

*So ought men to love their wives **as their own bodies**. He who loves his wife loves himself. **For no man ever yet hated his own flesh; but nourishes and cherishes it,** even as the Lord the church* (Ephesians 5:28-29).

It is NOT natural to hate your own body! *"For no man* [naturally] *ever yet hated his own flesh; but nourishes and cherishes it."* It takes religion to produce such self-hatred. Religion teaches what is against nature!

The negative view of self and our physical bodies is the religious act of *"the neglecting of the body."*

> *Wherefore if you are dead with Christ from the rudiments of the world, why, as though living in the world, are you subject to ordinances, (touch not; taste not; handle not; which all are to perish with the using;) after the commandments and doctrines of men? Which things have indeed a show of wisdom in will worship, and humility, **and neglecting of the body;** not in any honor to the satisfying of the flesh* (Colossians 2:20-23).

Religion, with its doctrines of men, is only a *show* of wisdom. It "looks good." It is showy – show business – but no matter how good it looks, it is against the design of God.

Don't neglect your body! It is not evil, depraved or wretched. It is God's handiwork. It's God's temple. Your body is His holy, acceptable sacrifice of glory, wonderfully made; and at the core of our bodies is our sexuality – male and female.

> *So God created man in His Own image, in the image of God created He him; **male and female created He them*** (Genesis 1:27).

Chapter 2

Commonness of Sexuality in the Bible

Sexual activity and expression was *much* more common to life in biblical times than anyone might be led to believe by religious tradition. Understanding this is of utmost importance in ultimately appreciating and honoring God with our own sexuality.

This chapter will help us to begin seeing a picture of how sexuality was viewed in biblical times. The purpose of this particular chapter simply is to give a brief overview of some of that commonness.

In this study we will bypass what would be so obvious to us in Scriptures. Instead, we will take a brief look at those parts of their common sexuality that, to us, may seem quite uncommon. You may be amazed that we will even look at some of these issues, but after all, we *are* people of "the Book." God has revealed and dealt with these topics, and we will have the spiritual courage to read and consider them. We will study for ourselves what God Himself has been bold enough to write about; but be forewarned, what follows may surprise you.

CIRCUMCISION

And you shall circumcise the flesh of your foreskin; and it shall be a token of the covenant between Me and you (Genesis 17:11).

God used the seat of man's sexuality, his penis, as a sign of His covenant with Abraham.

Just stop and think of it for a moment. Isn't that absolutely amazing? What a bold act by God. In His dealings with Israel, God focused attention on the male sex organ! If we were not so familiar with the story, we would surely insist it was extremely "vulgar" and "offensive!"

Circumcision should make it clear that men did not spend all of their time hiding their penises from others, for circumcision was a *sign* to someone. Others must have asked them, "What happened to your penis?"

ORIGINAL SPORT

And it came to pass, when he had been there a long time, that Abimelech king of the Philistines looked out at a window, and saw, and, behold, Isaac was sporting with Rebekah his wife (Genesis 26:8).

"Isaac was sporting with Rebekah his wife." What a sport! Isaac and Rebekah were seen having a playful sexual encounter in public! The king *"looked **out** at a window"* to see them. They obviously were not in a dead-bolt, locked-down room. They were outside engaged in marital enjoyment. Their society evidently did not have the same religious or "moral" view of sexuality that is so deeply rooted in ours.

PLURAL MARRIAGES

Then there is the great *hush-hush* of Bible reading and study – that of plural marriages. The Bible is filled with accounts of these. They were a very common style of family life in Bible times. In fact, many of God's greatest servants were clearly presented as having multiple wives.

We have been conditioned to push these accounts of plural marriages out of our consciousness as we read through the Bible – we just overlook them.

Were these plural marriages a sin? I have asked many students of the Scriptures about this – bringing the question into a modern setting. What would they do if they were in a polygamous society, say, among an African tribe? What if they were to lead a native man with many wives to trust in Christ? What would they instruct this new believer in Christ to do regarding his many wives? Would they instruct him to divorce and abandon all of his wives except for the first one, along with all of their children? Would not such a requirement be absurd? Those Bible students with whom I have spoken have agreed that it would be ridiculous.

The law of God given to Moses did not forbid multiple wives. The law did regulate almost every area of life, and polygamy was no exception. If polygamy was a sin, God would have forbidden it, rather than giving a law for its practice. Be assured that God has no problem communicating His disapproval of anything!

Beyond that, God even clearly required multiple marriages in some instances, which we shall consider later.

Polygamy is a *social* issue, not a *sin* issue.

BASIC EXAMPLES OF PROMINENT BIBLICAL CHARACTERS WHO HAD MULTIPLE WIVES

ABRAHAM

Abraham, the first Hebrew, and ancestor of all Israel, the father of all who believe (Romans 4:11-12), had three wives, namely Sarah and her servant Hagar (Genesis 16:3), and Keturah (Genesis 25:1), as well as a number of concubines (Genesis 25:6).

JACOB

Jacob, father of the twelve tribes of Israel had Rachel and Leah, who were sisters, as his wives (Genesis 29). He also was husband to their servants Bilhah and Zilpah (Genesis 30:4, 9). These bore him the twelve tribes of Israel. Without these four wives *there would be no Israel!* Plural marriage is at the foundation of God's establishment of the nation Israel.

MOSES

Moses was married to Zipporah, a Midianite (Exodus 2:21), and an unnamed Ethiopian (Numbers 12:1).

GIDEON

Gideon, a mighty man of God and judge of Israel, who defeated the Midianites, and whose name is now used in modern times by an organization to distribute Bibles worldwide, had 70 sons (and how many daughters?) because the Scripture says that he had *"many wives"* (Judges 8:30).

SAMUEL

Elkanah has two wives, Hannah and Peninah (I Samuel 1:2). Hannah gives birth to the prophet Samuel.

DAVID

King David, a man after God's own heart, had plenty of wives. God gave David all of his wives, and God clearly told him that if he wanted more, He would have given them to him (II Samuel 12:8).[1]

SOLOMON

Solomon had 700 wives and 300 concubines (I Kings 11:3). He wrote the Song of Solomon, a celebrated poem about marital love, to his 61st wife (Song of Solomon 6:8). Solomon's problem was that he ended up marrying ungodly foreign wives (*"strange women"*) who worshiped false gods, and turned his heart from the Lord; but go easy on Solomon. Some men have committed this *same sin* while married to only *one wife!*

---

1. It is amazing to discover the gems that are concealed in those Scripture passages – or parts of those Scripture passages – that we tend to ignore because they are overshadowed by other themes which are more "important" for our momentary purposes. An example can be found in Nathan's exposé of David's crime of adultery and murder. With it there was an endorsement of David's polygamy – and therefore polygamy in general.

REHOBOAM

Rehoboam had 18 wives and 60 concubines, making him another busy man with 28 sons and 60 daughters (II Chronicles 11:21).

God Himself a Polygamist

Amazingly, God even portrays Himself as being married to two sisters, Jerusalem and Samaria (Ezekiel 23:2-4; also see Jeremiah 3:6-10; 31:31-32, noting the phrase, *"I was a husband unto* **them***"*). Why would God use this analogy of multiple wives for Himself if it was sinful?

The Law regarding Polygamy

The Law had rules regulating polygamy and limiting its application under certain circumstances. For example, a man was not to marry his wife's sister, unless he had his wife's approval (Leviticus 18:18). Also, a man was not to marry both a woman and her mother (Leviticus 20:14). That would have presented confusing family ties. The very fact that these specific examples are banned shows the Mosaic Law's support of plural marriages.

Exodus 21:10 tells us that if a man marries an *additional* wife he must not deprive his current wife of her food, clothing and sexual pleasure. In other words, a man should not take more wives than he could provide for adequately.

Just like monogamy, polygamy surely had its fair share of problems, and the law intervened to make sure that the children received the inheritance to which they were entitled (Deuteronomy 21:15-17).

Polygamy was practiced without criticism in the Old Testament. It was legal and moral, and was clearly within the blessings of God. Indeed, the practice of marrying the wife of a deceased brother in order to ensure that the family line continued (Deuteronomy 25:5-6), and marrying an unengaged damsel with whom a man had had sex (Exodus 21:16) would have actually *required* such a man to have more than one wife, if he was already married.[2]

---

2. Thus the Scripture's expression, *"When a man has taken a* **new** *wife ..."* (Deuteronomy 24:5). The word *"new"* here is in contrast to "old," obviously a reference to the taking of an *additional* wife. The word *"new"* is translated *"fresh"* in Job 29:20 (*"châdâsh"* – Strong's *Hebrew Lexicon* #2319).

An Interesting Note from History

Some of the early reformers dealt with the issue of polygamy. In fact, the three leading figures of the German reformation, Luther, Melanchthon, and Bucer, signed the *Wittenberg Deliberation* which was mostly taken up with an examination of the biblical authority for polygamy. They jointly gave their public blessing to Philip the Magnanimous of Hesse to marry a second wife.

Luther contended that polygamy is not wrong, and definitely preferable to divorce. This was a position from which he never wavered.[3]

CONCUBINES

The English word concubine (from 'one to lie with' in Latin) translates the Hebrew *pilegesh*, a woman ... acquired by a man for his sexual pleasure, or to serve as a surrogate child-bearer ... The sons of concubines could inherit equally with those of wives, unless the father chose not to recognize them.[4]

Concubines are women who were provided headship in exchange for services, including sexual, as the word itself would suggest ("one to lie with"). Although this would seem strange to our Victorian-based society, this was simply an issue of compassionate and provisional extended headship, loving and tender sexuality, and normal biblical family life.

As with anything else, this practice could be, and undoubtedly was, abused. Nonetheless it was a great benefit to many women – primarily because headship and family life was extended. This biblical ethic was *far* superior to the modern one of the independent, headless female.

Concubinage is a form of polygamy in which the primary matrimonial relationship is supplemented by one or more secondary sexual relationships. Concubinage was a legally sanctioned and socially acceptable practice in ancient cultures, including that of the Hebrews ...[5]

3. John Cairncross, *After Polygamy Was Made A Sin: The Social History of Christian Polygamy,* 1974, London: Rouledge & Kegan Paul, pp. 33, 36, 49-50.
4. Ronald L. Ecker, *And Adam Knew Eve.*
5. Concubinage, *Funk & Wagnalls New Encyclopedia,* 1986, Funk & Wagnalls.

Although frequently their function was to provide sexual gratification ("man's delight," Ecclesiastes 2:8) they might also be given considerable responsibility.[6]

Handmaidens, given as a marriage gift, were also often concubines (e.g. Zilpah in Genesis 24:24, and Bilhah in Genesis 29:29). As such, therefore, they were protected by the Law (Exodus 21:7-11; Deuteronomy 21:10-14). Concubines were clearly distinguished from wives in Judges 8:31. The man provided headship and protection for his concubines.[7]

The biblical meaning was well understood for we read of a rather good definition from the 1563 Homilies: "After the phrase of the Scripture a concubine is an honest name."[8]

Concubinage, again, is scarcely an adulterous connection inasmuch it is ... a legitimate extension of conjugal rights to certain female members of a household, usually with the sanction of the true wife. Thus, in *practice* a concubine tends to become an additional wife in a polygamous establishment with an inferior status.[9]

Although the Bible is filled with references with concubinage, it is probably given even less conscious recognition by the reader of Scriptures than plural marriage. Here are some of the more famous Biblical characters who had concubines:

Abraham (Genesis 25:6)

Jacob (Genesis 35:22)

Gideon (Judges 8:30-31)

Caleb (I Chronicle 2:46)

David (II Samuel 5:13)

Solomon (I Kings 11:3)

Rehoboam (II Chronicles 11:21)

---

6. *Eerdman's Bible Dictionary*, p. 230.

7. *Eerdmans' New Bible Dictionary*, Editor J.D. Douglas; W.B. Eerdmans Publishing.

8. Stanislaw Królewiec, *Christian Concubines*, (internet article).

9. E.O. James, *Marriage Customs Through the Ages*, Collier Books, 1965, p. 179.

EROTICA IN THE BIBLE

In the Scriptures we find the literary artwork of sexual erotica. The Song of Solomon[10] is a prime example of such sexual passion expressed in the Bible. It contains the passion of a husband and his 61st wife, describing each other in their love-making. It is a very detailed and graphic presentation.

Based on the definition of "pornography" from the *American Heritage Dictionary,* parts of the Bible would surely be viewed as pornographic.[11] Song of Solomon demonstrates that such eroticism, in and of itself, is not sinful.

Why would God inspire such an erotic love story between a man and his wife? *There* is a question for the Victorian moralists! Of course their answer would be to allegorize the book, but even the allegory, it must be admitted, would have been based upon the love between a husband and wife.

We recognize that the more sexual content a writing has, the more it may arouse the reader. This is because sexual arousal – sometimes called passion – is an emotion.

Have you ever watched a scary movie and experienced the emotion of fear? Likewise, a story with sexual content causes the reader to experience the emotion of passion – or sexual desire.

As with any other passion, it is not a sin to experience the passion of sexual arousal. It could be a sin what you do with that passion, but that passion can be used to the glory of God. If married couples used the erotica found in the Bible (or elsewhere!) and applied their aroused passions to each other, this is not sin.

HARLOTS

Tamar

Regarding Tamar, T.J. Hornsby has written,

One of the implications of this story [Genesis 30] is that prostitutes seem to be

---

10. This Song is by the *young* Solomon, not the old Solomon who failed himself and his people by marrying foreign wives and concubines who didn't believe in Jehovah, the I Am of Sinai. This is the Solomon who was blessed and chosen of God to receive divine wisdom, build the great Temple and write many Scripture Proverbs.
11. "Sexually explicit pictures, writing, or other material ..."

a part of the landscape in ancient Israel… This story about prostitution, trickery and righteousness is an excellent reminder to us that, sometimes, those whom society judges as sexually immoral (in this case, Tamar) are the righteous ones.[12]

The Two Spies

The two spies of Israel spent days at the harlot Rahab's house (Joshua 2). What were they doing at a prostitute's house? Was this an appropriate place to lodge for men of God? Was their testimony at stake? Were they *"abstaining from the appearance of evil?"* Or dare we even have the courage to ask if they were using her other services?

Rahab

Again, T.J. Hornsby writes,[13]

> Some argue that the spies have no intention of having sex with Rahab the prostitute, but nearly every [basic] sexual euphemism of the Bible shows up in the first three verses of the passage [Joshua 2:1-3]: *"come in to,"*[14] *"enter,"*[15] *"lying with."*[16]

Samson

Samson was one of Israel's greatest judges. He is even listed in the "Hall of Faith" (Hebrews 11:32). Interestingly enough, he was full of the Spirit before and after (Judges 13:25; 14:6, 19; 15:14) he *"went in unto"* the harlot (Judges 16:1). Samson's sin with Delilah was not sexual, but one of confiding in an enemy of Israel – an idol-worshiping foreigner.

Solomon

Then there is that famous "Sunday School" account of Solomon's wisdom as

---

12. T.J. Hornsby, *Sex Texts from the Bible,* pp. 114, 116.
13. *Ibid.,* p. 120.
14. Come in to: *"came into"* (Strong's *Hebrew Lexicon* #935, "bow"). As an example, this word is translated euphemistically – just in Genesis – as *"come in unto"* in 6:4; 30:16; 38:16; 39:14; *"go in unto"* in 16:2; 28:21; 29:21; 30:3; 38:8; *"went in"* 19:33; 29:23, 30; 30:4; 38:2, 9.
15. Enter: "entered" (also the Hebrew word "bow" as in footnote 1).
16. Lying with: "lodged" (Strong's *Hebrew Lexicon* #7901, *shakab,* meaning "to lie down (for rest, sexual connection, decease or any other purpose). As an example, this word is translated euphemistically seven times in Genesis 19:32-35 alone as: *"we will lie"* with him, *"lay with,"* *"lay down,"* *"behold, I lay,"* *"and lie,"* *"and lay,"* *"when she lay down."*

recorded in I Kings 3:16-28. The funny thing is, I never remember hearing in Sunday School that these two women, who came to Solomon concerning their dispute, were harlots!

> *Then came there two women, **who were harlots,** unto the king, and stood before him* (I Kings 3:16).

> Two squabbling prostitutes … asked Solomon to settle a dispute. Noticeably absent in these narratives is any condemnation of their lifestyle. Solomon was in a position to have prostitutes executed, yet he allowed them to practice their trade without government interference.[17]

How common and accepted prostitution must have been in Biblical times!

There is no prohibition of harlotry under the law, in and of itself. The sole prohibition is to a father, *"Do not prostitute your daughter, to cause her to be a whore"* (Leviticus 19:29). This is an issue of the father's headship and covering over his daughter. Undoubtedly, harlotry was the profession of the headless, and such a legitimate and legal profession, that Solomon did not even address the issue. Harlotry's general condemnation in Scripture is in its association of pagan cultic worship of other gods.

To this Hornsby also concurs,

> The Bible speaks negatively about prostitution only when it is associated with worshipping other gods … It would be difficult, if not impossible, to find a biblical reference that tells men not to visit prostitutes.[18]

Jesus

Jesus preferred the presence of prostitutes over the legalistic religious leaders of His day. In fact, He said *they* would enter the kingdom ahead of them:

> *Jesus said unto them, "Verily I say unto you, that the publicans and the harlots go into the kingdom of God before you"* (Matthew 21:31).

He did *not* say "ex-harlots go into the kingdom of God before you."

---

17. Tom Gruber, *What the Bible Really Says About Sex, 2001,* Trafford Publishing, pp. 42, 44.
18. Hornsby, *Op. Cit.,* pp. 120, 124.

Sexually Suspect

Matthew's mention of Tamar, Bathsheba, Rahab and Ruth (1:1-17) reminds us that from the wombs of the sexually suspect come the greatest people of all.[19]

"Premarital" Sex[20]

Ruth and Boaz

Boaz, after Ruth had spent all night in his bed, decided he would like to marry her (Ruth chapter 3). What happened in that bed that night? The word "feet" is at times used as a euphemism.[21] Yet, even if this is not the case, what would a moralist think of such an account? Was it morally righteous for an unmarried man and woman to spend the night together in the same bed? Was such an act God-honoring? Was it a godly deed? Did she "abstain from all appearance of evil?" Or, were they not wound as tight as the religious legalists from the "moral majority?"

Tom Shipley writes:

> What then is the meaning of Naomi's advice to Ruth to *"uncover his feet and lay thee down?"* … There is only one possible meaning. Naomi advised Ruth to seduce Boaz into sexual relations as a means of securing him as her kinsman redeemer. After exposing Boaz's "feet," that is, his private parts, Ruth was then to *"lay thee down."* Consider the sequence: first to expose Boaz's nakedness and then to lie down. This sequence of acts is nothing else, and can be nothing else, except a direct invitation to sexual intercourse. Boaz could not possibly have mistaken the meaning and significance of Ruth's actions.[22]

---

19. *Ibid., p. 110.*
20. "The issue of whether sex outside of marriage is advisable is a different question. We seek only to find whether God defines it as sin. Our studied opinion is that He does not so define it … The Bible does not contain a law, and example, or a word that designates sexual activity by single people. Therefore it is impossible to honestly state that 'The Bible condemns sex by single people.'" – Philo Thelos, *Divine Sex: Liberating Sex from Religious Tradition,* 2002, p. 155.
21. "… Feet being a euphemism for genitalia …" Ecker, *Op. Cit.*

    "'Feet' [here used] to replace the word phallus." Robert W. Stace, *Why Weren't We Told?* 2001, p. 75. "Biblical euphemism for the genitals … The ancient audience would have recognized the term as implying that Ruth actually seduced Boaz." David Biale, *Eros and the Jews,* 1993, pp. 14-15.

    "The expression [feet] is used for private acts in Scripture … Private parts of the human anatomy, below the waist, were called 'feet,' and … 'uncovering the feet' refers to sexual relations …" – James Jordan, *Judges: God's War Against Humanism,* pp. 63, 65.
22. Tom Shipley, *Man and Woman in Biblical Law: A Patriarchal Manifesto (They Shall Be One Flesh, Part II),* 2009, p. 23.

Philo Thelos agrees:

> "Uncover the feet" was a well known euphemism in that culture for "expose the genitals." Moffatt translates the Hebrew words this way: "*uncover his waist and lay down there.*" She was advised to uncover Boaz's genitals and lay down beside him. When he woke up with his genitals uncovered and Ruth lying beside him, he did not have to guess what she wanted! She was offering herself to him sexually, and he was willing! When she asked him to "*spread your covering over me*" she used a euphemism for sexual intercourse. This phrase arose because in sexual intercourse, a woman lying on her back lays open her robe to the man. The man spreads his robe apart as he lies on top of her, Thus the phrase "*cover with my robe* (or skirt, or covering)" also came to refer to sexual intercourse.[23]

THE AROUSAL OF OLD MEN

> *Now king David was old and stricken in years; and they covered him with clothes, but he got no heat. Wherefore his servants said unto him, "Let there be sought for my lord the king a young virgin: and let her stand before the king, and let her cherish him, and let her lie in your bosom, that my lord the king may get heat." So they sought for a fair damsel throughout all the coasts of Israel, and found Abishag a Shunammite, and brought her to the king. And the damsel was very fair, and cherished the king, and ministered to him: but the king knew her not (I Kings 1:1-4).*

Now here is an amazing account recorded for our attention by God. When David was dying, the most beautiful virgin of the kingdom was selected for him to help arouse him in hopes of stimulating his body functions and get him warmed up!

One author writes,

> How did David's court determine the king was dying? They brought a young beautiful woman ... When he did not respond, they knew David's time was running out. Many people give up on life long before they should.[24]

Another author writes,

> Obviously it is the sexual excitement that would increase the "*heat*" so David

---

23. Philo Thelos, Op. Cit. p. 25.
24. Earl Paulk, *Sex Is God's Idea*, K Dimension Publishers, Atlanta, GA, 1985, p. 155.

would be warm … The natural body of even an extremely beautiful woman would provide no more physical "warmth" than any of the wives and concubines already had. It is the added sexual "heat" that they count on to warm David.[25]

Hornsby adds;

> Passages like this [I Kings 1:1-4] show us that sexual "heat" is recognized, even in the Bible, as having some sort of healing benefits.[26]

THE SEXUAL NEEDS OF SERVANTS

If you buy a Hebrew servant, six years he shall serve: and in the seventh he shall go out free for nothing. If he came in by himself, he shall go out by himself: if he was married, then his wife shall go out with him. If his master has given him a wife, and she has born him sons or daughters; the wife and her children shall be her master's, and he shall go out by himself (Exodus 21:2-4).

This passage shows the loving provision that God made for the sexual needs of men. Slaves would not have had the financial means to acquire a wife, so the master was permitted by the sanction of God to lend him the use of one of the women under his headship for the duration of his service, and it is clear that this meant the reality of a possible pregnancy.

Later, when it was time for the servant to go free, he was to give back to his master – their rightful head – the woman and any possible children born out of this union. This was all done with the permission and provision of the very law of God! This was not adultery, as it was done with the permission of the master (head). Therefore, as we can see from this passage, not *all* non-husband and non-wife sexual relations are sinful. Sexual relations with permission of headship, which do not involve betrayal, are *not* classified as adultery and can be honorable before God.

QUEEN ESTHER

The whole story related to Queen Esther has long perplexed the reader of Scripture. What exactly was going on? Was there not a clear sexual undertone to this whole story?

25. Philo Thelos, *Op. Cit.,* p. 79.
26. Hornsby, *Op. Cit.,* p. 42.

One writer sheds some light,

> Isn't it about time we realized that not only was sex God's idea, but God also
> used sex to influence kingdoms and change lives for good? Nothing less than
> a combination of obedience and sexuality gave Esther half the kingdom and
> saved the Jews from destruction.[27]

FEMALE INTIMACIES

Martin Zender observes,

> This will shock some of you: Women lying with women were not stoned under
> the Law of Moses. I didn't believe this myself until I looked it up. Leviticus
> 20 lists the sexual sins; check it out. Adultery is a capital offense, and so is a
> man lying with his mother, or his daughter, or any number of female family
> members. Verse 13 condemns men penetrating other men: *"If a man also lie
> with mankind, as he lieth with a woman, both of them have committed an
> abomination; they shall surely be put to death."* The next verse warns against
> sex with mothers-in-law (not a problem for most men), and verse 15 administers
> death to a man who lies with a beast. Women receive the same warning in the
> next verse, verse 16.
>
> So where is the verse keeping women apart? IT ISN'T HERE. Why? Because
> women cannot penetrate one another. There is something physically and
> spiritually serious about where the male member of both man and beast
> ventures. In 1 Cor. 6:16, a man who joins a prostitute becomes one body with
> her. Is he joining her for dinner? No. He is physically joining her; the issue is
> penetration.
>
> Paul writes in 1 Cor. 11:14 that *"nature itself teaches you"* that long hair on a
> man is dishonorable, but on a woman it is glorious. It's the same with female
> intimacies. Females can dance together, cuddle, and comb one another's
> hair, and even grandmother says, "Oh, that is so nice." Let the above happen
> among boys and see how granny reacts. The lesson? Here is my guess: Female
> intimacies show us something of the beauty and gentleness of God.[28]

---

27. Paulk, *Op. Cit.,* p. 2.
28. Martin Zender, *Clanging Gong News,* 2009, Vol. 1 No. 23.

DUE BENEVOLENCE

Let the husband render unto the wife due benevolence: and likewise also the wife unto the husband. The wife has not power of her own body, but the husband: and likewise also the husband has not power of his own body, but the wife. Defraud not one the other, except it be with consent for a time, that you may give yourselves to fasting and prayer; and come together again, that Satan tempts you not for your incontinency (I Corinthians 7:3-5).

Marital sex is a God-ordained ministry. The husband and wife should be creative, zealous and devoted in their sexual ministry to each other. Paul only gives one reason for abstinence from this ministry: fasting and prayer! The way some couples refrain from this ministry, they must be attempting to break the fasting record! In fact, if this single reason for marital abstinence were actually followed, many couples would be dead of starvation! Paul's instruction seems clear: no sex, no food![29]

MASTERS, SERVANTS AND SEX

Both of the apostles Peter and Paul had clear instructions for those who were slaves. This may have little impact upon the modern reader as he reads these instructions. We are far removed from their implications. Thoughtfully consider the background perspective presented by a contemporary author.

In the days of the Bible, "slaves were traded freely and became the property of their owners. …

"It was a common requirement for a slave woman to share her sexual favors with her master and his sons. …

"Although it was a minor offense to have sex with another man's slave, the same action was customary if the slave owner gave his permission. One was stealing, the other was graciously accepting an act of hospitality. Men had a right to share what was theirs."[30]

Moving to the New Testament, there were six million slaves in the Roman Empire alone. Considering many of the early Christians were slaves, one might

---

29. Obviously physical sickness or inability would be legitimate reasons for the loss of physical union.
30. Epstein, L.M., *Sex Laws and Customs in Judaism,* New York: KTAV Publishing, 1967. Cited by Tom Gruber, *Op. Cit.,* pp. 49-51.

wonder how they were expected to conduct their sexual lives. Hypothetically, let's say an early female Christian slave was having sexual relations with her master, her master's sons, and her master's neighbors. Such a hypothetical situation was not only possible, it was probable. Would Paul expect this Christian slave woman to defy her master by refusing ...? To withhold her sexual obligations would have been considered robbing her master of what was rightfully his.

What advice did Paul give? Slaves were instructed to serve their masters wholeheartedly,

> *Servants, be obedient to them who are your masters according to the flesh, with fear and trembling, in singleness of your heart, as unto Christ; Not with eyeservice, as menpleasers; but as the servants of Christ, doing the will of God from the heart; With good will doing service, as to the Lord, and not to men: Knowing that whatsoever good thing any man does, the same shall he receive of the Lord, whether he is bond or free (Ephesians 6:5-8).*

Peter says the same thing,

> *Servants, be subject to your masters with all fear; not only to the good and gentle, but also to the froward (I Peter 2:18).*

Peter instructed slaves to submit to their masters, even if their masters were bad ... Although sexual matters are not specifically addressed here, this must have been a concern. Nowhere does Peter or Paul tell slaves to refuse conjugal duties with their masters. This would have been their obligation, and an act of submission to Christ.

Considering the nature of slavery, an infinite number of hypothetical situations must have arisen. Put yourself in Paul's position, giving advice to these slaves. What if a ... slave woman has recently been traded? Naturally, her new owner expects her to [among other things] ... satisfy him sexually. This was [in part] why he purchased her. Scripture indicates both Peter and Paul would advise her to obey her master and give him his conjugal duties.[31]

---

31. Gruber, *Op. Cit.*, 2001, pp. 49-51.

THE MARRIAGE BED

Marriage is honorable in all, and the bed undefiled: but whoremongers and adulterers God will judge (Hebrews 13:4).

The marriage bed is honorable!

The word "bed" in Hebrews 13:4 is a euphemism for sex (the act of marriage). The Greek word for bed here is *koitē* from which we get the word "coitus" (which means sexual intercourse). It is Strong's *Greek Lexicon #2845*, of which he says, "by implication, the male sperm." Thayer defines the word as "sexual intercourse."[32]

What God will judge is adultery and fornication (whoremonger[33] is the Greek word "*pornos*" which is translated *fornication*)! We will talk about adultery and fornication in detail later!

A BIBLE FILLED WITH SEX!

What is our conclusion from this brief look at some of the content of the Bible? We have a Bible *filled* with sex! There was clearly a different mindset in Biblical times. There is a different mindset by God. What seems so unusual to us was commonplace within their setting.

Our religious society has mastered the art of calling *"evil good, and good evil"* (Isaiah 5:20). In one sweeping motion, they have taken God's wonderful gift of sexuality and almost uniformly called it evil.

---

32. *A Greek-English Lexicon of the New Testament,* Joseph H. Thayer, Grand Rapids, MI, Baker, 1995.
33. "Monger" is a suffix meaning "dealer." A whoremonger is a pimp.

Chapter 3

The Biblical Purpose of Sexuality

"Of sex is an expression of love, then Christians, above all people, should take a special delight in it."[1]

Over the centuries scores have been raised with the teaching that sexuality, in and of *itself*, is sinful. "Church history" literally is filled with teachers who have gone so far as to teach that it was wrong even to have a sexual encounter with one's own spouse.

Sex does, however, have a number of clearly designed godly purposes. Two of the most obvious purposes of sexual activity should be bonding and procreation. Both of these purposes are very important. The Bible places special emphasis upon both of these aspects.

Bonding

Therefore shall a man leave his father and his mother, and shall cleave unto his wife: and they shall be one flesh. And they were both naked, the man and his wife, and were not ashamed (Genesis 2:24-25).

---

1. Gordon Thomas, *Desire and Denial,* Brown and Little, 1986, p. 29.

Procreation

> *And God blessed them, and God said unto them, "Be fruitful, and multiply, and replenish the earth"* (Genesis 1:28).

Bonding and procreation are met, ideally, by the design of God in the husband-wife relationship.[2] How gracious and wonderful our Lord was to make such a provisional plan.

Pleasure

Nevertheless, one often would be led to believe that bonding and procreation are the *only* legitimate purposes of sex. This could not be further from the truth! Pleasure is another important purpose of sex, as God designed it. God designed sex not only to bond and have the potential of producing offspring, but also to provide pleasure – to be intensely enjoyable! Thank God for His amazing bounty, *"Who gives us richly all things to enjoy"* (I Timothy 6:17).

In the Bible there is abundant evidence to this fact. There is also evidence to this fact in human anatomy. Almost anyone who has engaged in positive sexual activity can attest to the wonderful pleasure our benevolent Creator has provided.

There is an acknowledgment by some in Christendom that bonding and procreation are indeed divine purposes of sexuality. However, there is usually a reluctance to recognize or admit the purpose of godly pleasure. Christendom provides endless sermons and literature against sex – on the *sins* of sexuality – but rarely, *if ever*, does it provide sermons or literature about the positive aspect of sex – on the *godly* pleasures of sex. Therefore, *sexual pleasure* is the main subject of thought in this chapter.

Have you ever thought why sex would feel so good? If it was just about bonding and procreation, why would it have such powerful feelings? The answer is quite simple: because God designed it so! He wanted mankind to enjoy the repeated pleasure of sexual release! What a Creator we worship! Sadly, we hear little of this aspect of our glorious Lord.

---

2. We say, "ideally," but not always. Let us offer an example. The greatest birth in history was when a child was fathered by someone who was NOT married to his mother! We speak here of the blessed birth of the Lord Jesus Christ. God fathered a child by a woman who was not His wife. This was a surrogate conception.

David M. Freeman states concerning the historical Jewish view,

> In Jewish history coitus has been consistently and unambiguously valued for the sheer joy and pleasure of it, even where procreation was obviously impossible.[3]

Although sexual pleasure is associated with bonding and procreation, it is in fact a distinctly separate issue, which is made clear from Scripture, nature and our own experience.

> God has given us sex for more than just the creation of babies. Sex is also given to people for recreation. It is a resource, a way to take our minds away from harsh realities of daily life. The experience surrounds us and brings us into a human relationship that yields warmth, understanding and acceptance.[4]

Think with me briefly about the three areas of Scripture, nature, and experience.

Scripture

Many verses attest to the pure pleasurable aspect of sex. Here are two such passages:

> *Drink waters out of your own cistern, and running waters out of your own well. Let your fountains[5] be dispersed abroad, and rivers of waters in the streets. Let them be only your own, and not strangers' with you. Let your fountain be blessed: and **rejoice** with the wife of your youth. Let her be as the loving hind and pleasant roe; let her breasts **satisfy** you at all times; and be **ravished** [intoxicated] always with her love (Proverbs 5:15-19).*

> *You have **ravished** my heart, my sister, my spouse; you have **ravished** my heart with one of your eyes, with one chain of your neck. How fair is your love, my sister, my spouse! how much better is your love than wine! and the smell of your ointments than all spices! Your lips, O my spouse, drop as the honeycomb: honey and milk are under your tongue; and the smell of your garments is like the smell of Lebanon. A garden inclosed is my sister,*

---

3. David M. Feldman, *Marital Relations,* Schocken Books.
4. Earl Paulk, *Sex Is God's Idea,* K Dimension Publishers, Atlanta, GA, 1985, p. 155.
5. "Graze on my lips; and if those hills be dry, stray lower, where the pleasant fountains lie." – William Shakespeare, *Venus and Adonis.*

my spouse; a spring shut up, a fountain sealed. Your plants are an orchard of pomegranates, with pleasant fruits; camphire, with spikenard, Spikenard and saffron; calamus and cinnamon, with all trees of frankincense; myrrh and aloes, with all the chief spices. A fountain of gardens, a well of living waters, and streams from Lebanon. Awake, O north wind; and come, you south; blow upon my garden, that the spices thereof may flow out. Let my beloved come into his garden, and eat his pleasant fruits (Song of Solomon 4:9-16).

This later passage, from the *Song of Solomon*, was written obviously with the clear intention of being provocative and sensuous. You can see this by the descriptions that mention the breasts and their beauty, and how the girl was described as a fragrant garden of fruits and scents. Then she "invites" him to come to his garden and "eat" its choicest "fruits."

If one is unfamiliar with the Hebrew words used in the passages, a simple study would reveal an even stronger erotic nature of these passages than might be understood from our English translation.

Nature

Nature will point to the pleasurable design of sex. Look at the female anatomy for example. The female finds sexual pleasure in *many* parts of her body. Take the dual role of her breasts for instance. They can be used to nurture, comfort, and bond with an infant, but also to pleasure a man (both by sight and contact!), and bring great sexual pleasure to herself as well.

Now, some would attempt to argue that this pleasure is purely secondary, if not actually carnal. They will insist that the main function of the breasts is the feeding of infants. This absolutely is *not* the case, and can be so demonstrated from the Bible and from experience as well.

If the sole purpose of the female breasts are to nurture children, why then does the female have them for all of her adult life? Why does she not have them just at lactating periods of her life? Or, why does a woman who never has had children have them in the first place?

The fact is, the female breasts have a number of purposes besides child feeding! As mentioned before, they pleasure the sight of men, satisfy the sexual needs of men, and bring sexual pleasure to the woman as well! The breasts have a basic dual purpose: nutrition and sex! Godly women can put *both* of these divine aspects to work! They can make good and godly use of what God has given them![6]

All this aside, let us consider *another* female body part that has *only* one known purpose. If pleasure is not one of the purposes of sex, then what is the purpose of the female clitoris? It has only one known purpose. It is a button of sexual pleasure! It is a part of the female body designed for the sole purpose of pleasure! Think of it! What a Creator! He specifically designed and built the women to have intense sexual pleasure. Right in the woman's body is the evidence of His handiwork designed purely for her sexual pleasure!

Moreover, what about *female* ejaculation? What is the purpose of the female's *"running waters?"*[7] Are most husbands and wives even ignorant of the powerfully pleasurable *female* ejaculation? Although it is possible that many women have been deprived of this feminine ability by ignorance, it is for others a strongly orgasmic experience which the Bible openly discusses. What purpose other than sexual delight does it have? Some may attempt to argue that male ejaculation has not as its main purpose sexual pleasure, but the delivery of the seed of procreation, but one could not attempt to make such an argument for female ejaculation.

Other Considerations

Let's move on to other considerations. Take **masturbation.** Here is a very natural means of sexual enjoyment, one which the Bible (even the Law of Moses) does not condemn, nor even regulate. What is the purpose of masturbation, or sexual self-pleasure? It is not procreation. It is not bonding. Here again we find an example of sexual activity for the very pleasure it brings, and this can be good and healthy (physically, emotionally and mentally)!

Many well-meaning Christians would attempt to make this out to be a sinful act. Where is the clear teaching of Scripture that such a universally common act is sinful? God is so abundantly clear and straightforward in His prohibitions of sin. If such a common activity were sinful, would He not have clearly addressed it?

---

6. Speaking of the pleasurable sight of the female bosom, if this was not the intended purpose of God, why did He ornament the woman with them right up front in such an obviously noticeable place? They are *unavoidable!* They could have been placed in a far less prominent place, made mostly internal with only the nipple external, or had a retractable function, but the Creator gave them a very conspicuous, prominent place. Did He do so to tempt man and give him endless struggles, battles and grief? Or was it a part of His gracious provision for man? Oh, the beauty of the female form! He wants us to take pleasure in His creation! We honor the Creator when we do!

7. Study the neglected passage of Proverbs 5:15-19.

Those free from the tyranny of religious thought have no scruples about such an honorable, godly release.

One author has insightfully written,

> If masturbation is sinful where is the Biblical law that says so? How can a sexual practice that involves no one but the practitioner, be evil? And when does that evil begin? Has the small child sinned when (s)he discovers that touching the genitals feels good? ... Is the "sinfulness" of masturbation determined by one's age? Or by how often one ouches one's genitals? Or by how much pleasure one derives for the practice? If it is sinful, how do we actually *know* that, and what exactly is it that *makes* it a "sin"?[8]

Take **oral sex.** Dr. Herbert Miles, in his book *Sexual Happiness in Marriage*, quotes from a letter he received from a husband in favor of oral sex in Christian marriages. The writer states that, in his opinion, wherever you use your fingers to caress your wife's body, it is allowable to use your tongue. The writer believes that if you say that it is alright to kiss your wife's breasts and body but not alright to kiss genitals, you're categorizing her genitals as dirty or inferior. This, he believes, is contrary to what the Bible says about our bodies – that our bodies are *"fearfully and wonderfully made ..."* (Psalm 139:14).[9]

Onanism

One passage that often is used to condemn masturbation is the "sin of Onan" as recorded in Genesis 38:8-10. Onan's sin was actually the refusal to satisfy the principle of the Levirate law (Deuteronomy 25:5-10). This law required that a man marry and provide offspring for his deceased brother's wife. The latter part Onan refused to do. This sin had to do with headship – his refusal to take family responsibility.[10] It has nothing whatsoever to do with masturbation!

David McKay notes,

> One of the cleverest ways the church has ever found to control the masses has been to make masturbation a sin. The consequence has been that the

---

8. Philo Thelos, *Divine Sex: Liberating Sex from Religious Tradition,* 2002, p. v.
9. Louis S. Greenup, Jr., *How To Stop the Other Woman from Stealing Your Husband,* 1998, pp. 100-101.
10. As an interesting side note, if the living brother was already married, the Levirate law would also have required him to become a polygamist. How differently God views things!

most dishonest (*i.e.*, the ones who try to give the impression that they don't masturbate) are looked on as being the most holy, while more genuine believers are made to feel guilty and in need of absolution from the hypocrites.[11]

A Fourth Purpose

We have briefly mentioned the purpose of bonding and procreation, but it has been the goal of this chapter to focus upon the neglected purpose of pleasure. Yet, ultimately, there is a fourth purpose of sex that transcends all others, giving glory to God.

> *Whether therefore you eat, or drink, or whatsoever you do, do all to the glory of God* (I Corinthians 10:31).

As believers, every area of our lives belongs to God. We have the joy, privilege and opportunity of living every detail, of every moment, of every day for His glory. *"Whatsoever you do"* certainly includes our sex lives. This part of our lives can also be lived as a means of worshipping God.

Allowing God passage to live His *own* life through the *everyday* details of life is the only way to have real and *lasting* purpose in life. This divine life flows through the most *basic* elements of our lives – not the least of which is sex. We should glorify and worship God in our sexuality!

Foundational Purpose of Sex

So we have four foundational purposes for sex: bonding, procreation, pleasure and bringing glory to God. For the believer, the last purpose is paramount and should *always* be present in our lives, regardless of what we are doing; but not all of the first three are necessarily present at the same time. In fact, rarely are all three present at the same time! All three being valid, any one of these alone *could* be sufficient reason to engage in sexual activity, and such engagement *should* also bring glory to God. Any one of them *can* do so as long as no definite sin is involved – sin as defined by God.[12]

That being the case, it is possible that one *can* have sex for the pure pleasure of it, without intending to bond, or have children. Setting aside for a moment – if we

---

11. David McKay, *Air Travelers Magazine*, Vol. VII.

12. Sins such as defrauding others (adultery and rape), confusing of family headship (incest), and worshiping false gods (fornication and going after "strange women").

can – our own prejudiced social and religious customs, from a purely Biblical stand-point, who might a man have sex with, just for the sheer pleasure of having sex?

1. Himself
2. His wife(s)
3. His concubine(s)
4. His handmaid(s)
5. His servant(s)
6. Someone else's "woman"[13] with their permission
7. An unbetrothed virgin
8. A non-cultic prostitute

Although all of these may not always be an ideal form of sexual conduct, depending on specific circumstances and culture; nevertheless we must face this issue honestly with the divine standard provided for us by the Scriptures themselves. Regardless of how any of these may seem to us, no other standard will do.

We shall look at these more carefully from the Scripture as we develop these themes biblically; but for the moment, let's take a quick look at some "recognized" Christian resources.

Ancient Societies

Old Testament Professor David M. Carr writes,

> As in many ancient societies, both married and unmarried Israelite men were free to have sex with prostitutes, war prisoners, and any other unmarried, non-protected women they wished.[14]

The Hebrew's Positive View of Sex

David R. Mace, respected author of marriage books asserts,

> The Hebrews had a very positive view of sex. All who read the Old Testament must notice at once how openly and naturally the subject is treated ... The Hebrew view set some limitations on sexual freedom. Incest and rape were punishable offenses.[15]

---

13. Such is the case of the law dealing with the sexual needs of servants.
14. David M. Carr, *The Erotic Word,* Oxford University Press, 2003, p. 53.
15. David R. Mace, *The Sacred Fire,* Abingdon Press, 1986, pp. 31, 32.

Unger's Bible Dictionary, published by **Moody Press,** states:

> He [the husband] might have more wives than one, or have intercourse with a person not espoused or married to him, without being considered an adulterer.
> …

Baker's Evangelical Dictionary of Biblical Theology, under the listing of Immorality, Sexual, states:

> A man was not considered an adulterer if he engaged in sexual relations with a female slave (Genesis 16:1-4), a prostitute (Genesis 38:15-18), or his wife's handmaid with the spouse's permission (Genesis 16:4). Nor was a man deemed to be in an adulterous relationship if he happened to be married to two wives.

Yet another well-known source declares,

> To the husband was granted much more liberty. Although he also was forbidden to commit adultery with another man's wife, he was allowed to increase the number of his own wives and concubines, according to his desires and means, and also to have intercourse with women outside of his own house, provided only that these were not already bound by betrothal or by a completed marriage. In case he violated a still free virgin, he was dealt with according to the law in Exodus 22:15; Deuteronomy 22:28ff. What a wife was entitled to demand from a husband is told in Exodus 21:10. We nowhere read anything to the effect that he was forbidden extramarital intercourse with other women.[16]

HONORING GOD WITH SEXUAL ENJOYMENT

One bold author declares,

> A study of all God's laws regarding sex reveals His basic concern. God was not afraid of sex or fearful that His people might actually enjoy sex.

> The erotic joy and power inherent in sexuality is by God's wonderful design. God expects us to enjoy sex. We honor God when we thrill at sexual pleasure.[17]

---

16. *A New Standard Bible Dictionary,* Marriage and Divorce, Funk & Wagnalls, 1926.
17. Philo Thelos, *Op. Cit.,* p. 161.

Chapter 4

"Who Told Thee That Thou Wast Naked?"

A Look at Nudity in the Bible

And He said, "Who told you that you were naked? Have you eaten of the tree, whereof I commanded you that you should not eat?" (Genesis 3:11).

Many people have been brought up with the teaching that nudity (partial or full), in and of *itself*, is morally wrong, and that we should never allow others to see our bodies. Throughout "church history" some teachers have gone so far as to teach that it was wrong even to see one's self, or one's spouse naked.

Just how much of our bodies can be seen will depend upon the particular religious and social culture and subculture of one's own generation. Early last century it was a social norm in many circles to have women covered from the neck with high collars, to the ankles and wrists, with a bonnet on the head, revealing little more than the face and hands (and even then veils and gloves were often used).

As believers, we are not simply to allow contemporary society and culture to provide our understanding of what is, or is not right before God. The simple fact is that nudity does not have an inborn sense of shame: it is learned behavior. Babies have no shame, and neither did many in Biblical times. Nudity (partial or full) was common to the days of Scripture. Let us take a brief look through the Scriptures themselves.

Adam and Eve

God created Adam and Eve naked and unashamed (Genesis 2:25), a situation that He said was *"good."* God is not ashamed of our nudity (Hebrews 4:13). The body is a masterpiece of beauty, and should be admired as the handiwork of our gracious Creator (Psalm 139:14).

It is *sin* that actually distorted Adam and Eve's view of nudity. Why did Adam all-of-a-sudden become so conscious of his nudity? Did he not know that he was naked before? It was SIN that caused Adam and Eve to be *self-conscious* regarding nudity. Sin taints the conscience and leads us to an attitude of preoccupation to cover up and hide – even our own bodies (Genesis 3:7-8).

Sin affected their so-called "moral" view, thus having a direct effect upon their marriage relationship. Now Adam and Eve felt the need to have clothing even with each other. Think of it – no one else was around – nothing had changed, except their perception. Sin had defiled Adam's conscience. This is why Paul said,

> *Unto the pure all things are pure: but unto them who are defiled and unbelieving is nothing pure; but even their mind and conscience is defiled* (Titus 1:15).

Adam now was defiled, and viewed even his naked body – made by God – as shameful. Solomon said that *"the plowing of the wicked, is sin"* (Proverbs 21:4). This is the state in which Adam was now found.

Adam – unclear, unforgiven, and with a guilty conscious – covered his God-made nakedness with a garment of man-made fig leaves (Genesis 3:7-8). God's action of providing animal skins was in response to Adam and Eve's own actions.[1] Clothing was in fact God's merciful provision related to *physical* necessity, NOT *moral* necessity. Man needed clothing for protection from the elements, for God was driving man out of the garden into a hostile environment of thorns and thistles (Genesis 3:17-19, 23-24).

---

1. If all nudity (partial or full) must be covered (in some or all circumstances) based upon this passage, then aren't we disobeying God's supposedly inferred Word by not covering ourselves with animal skins? Why do we cover ourselves with cotton (a product of the ground like the fig leaves!), and polyester (and other man-made materials)?

   Furthermore, if all nudity (partial or full) must be covered based upon this passage, then husbands and wives should be clothed even when they are alone – for it was just the two of them in the garden.

Circumcision

Amazingly, God used the male penis as a sign (Romans 4:11; Genesis 17:10-14) that Jewish people were His chosen people. Stop and reflect on this. Doesn't that seem out of character with religious morality?

To whom was this mark on the male sex organ a *sign*? It would seem to us that the *sign of circumcision* must have revealed a truth to someone. Doesn't this demonstrate that they were not obsessed with keeping their penises covered all the time?

For example, we know from history that it was a common practice for the ancients to bathe nude in rivers and lakes. In fact, don't we bathe in the nude? They did not have the modern accommodations of indoor plumbing. They did it outside, making use of the provisions that God had made. It was natural. They also fished in the nude and played sports in the nude. It was during times such as these that they would have naturally been asked by others, "What's the deal with your penis?"

We must stop reading contemporary social customs, morals and culture into everything. We must come to grips with the fact that traditional Western society has an unusual and unnatural view (in relationship to much of the rest of human history) concerning nudity and many areas of sexuality.

Dancing David

Have we forgotten that David danced naked before the Lord, exposing himself to others in the process? Did you ever stop to think why God would even tell us this? God did not even condemn or punish David for his nude dancing. God did, however, punish Michal, one of his wives, making her childless for criticizing David for exposing himself to his handmaidens (II Samuel 6:20-23). Don't we view this as extremely odd? Then again, maybe our own views are what is odd and unusual.[2]

Bathing Bathsheba

David stood on the roof of his palace, and saw Bathsheba taking a bath (II Samuel 11:2). Did anyone ever wonder why **Bath**sheba took a bath in such a visible place,

---

2. "For one to dance naked for admiring crowds is no more immoral now, than it was for the Shulammite girl to dance naked for admiring onlookers in the Song of Solomon ..." – Philo Thelos, *Divine Sex: Liberating Sex from Religious Tradition*, 2002, p. 140.

knowing that there was the possibility for her to be seen, unless this was a common practice?

David's sin was not that he had looked at, or even admired Bathsheba's beauty, but that he sought and conspired to take that which *did not belong to him* (the sin of adultery). Interestingly, God's response to David's sin of adultery with Bathsheba was that if David had too few wives, He would have given him more (II Samuel 12:7-8ff).

According to Adam Clarke's Commentary,

> In town, pools of water are to be seen everywhere, and women may be seen morning and evening bathing in them, and carrying water home. Thus David might have seen Bathsheba, and no blame attached to her.

This passage affords us an interesting glimpse of life in ancient Israel.

The Shulamite Striptease

> A positive example of biblical burlesque has, as its main attraction, a beautiful Shulamite girl (Song of Solomon 6:13-7:9). As she struts her stuff, the crowd cries out for her to dance their way so they can get a better view. All she is wearing is her shoes and a smile … Her nude body was clearly visible to her attentive audience. And her lover fully approved.[3]

Prophets in the Nude

Although few Bible readers even realize it, the Jewish prophets of the Old Testament were commonly naked, so much so that when Saul stripped off his clothes and prophesied naked the people figured he *must* be a prophet (I Samuel 19:24). Amazingly, Isaiah prophesied in the nude for three years (Isaiah 20:2-3). We missed that one in Sunday school.

Testi-Fying

Many Bible readers fail to observe the fact that touching the testicles of a patriarch was a way of "testifying" to the validity of his statement or vow. This was true in Hebrew, Greek and Roman customs. Have you ever seen or considered the

---

3. Tom Gruber, *What the Bible Really Says About Sex,* Trafford Publishing, 2001, pp. 33-35.

connection between the word *testify* and *testicle*? The fact is, our words testify, testimony and testament have come from the word *testes* (see *"thigh"* in Genesis 24:2, 9; 47:29).[4]

When we read passages like these, doesn't it seem so very odd? We can't even imagine placing our hands under a man's testicles to swear or testify. We place our hand on the Bible to testify solemnly. The male penis was the ancients' version of "the Bible" testimony. When and how did "the Bible" replace "the testicles" in the swearing practice?

It is "our" society that has such hang-ups that make it almost impossible for us to think of such a practice as *even* being possible. We are not advocating here that we return to this practice of giving testimony. We are simply using it as an example of how skewed our "modern" understanding really is. It is amazing that such simple things from the Bible pose such serious concerns to our way of thinking.

Seizing a Man's "Private Parts"

*When men strive together one with another, and the wife of the one draws near for to deliver her husband out of the hand of him who smites him, and puts forth her hand, and takes him by the **secrets** (Deuteronomy 25:11).*

---

4. The etymology of the word "testis" is confirmed by all major resources (such as Oxford, Barnhart, Partridge, etc.) "Diminutive of testis in testiculus ... from the early practice of placing the hand on the seat of manliness when swearing: the *King James Bible* calls it the hand on the thigh." – Joseph T. Shipley, *Dictionary of Word Origins.*

"In the Bible, the lower extremities (thighs, feet, legs) can be euphemisms for genitalia." -- Charles J. Wilhelm, *Biblical Dyslexia* (2004), p. 80.

"This is puzzling language until you realize that 'thigh' was often used by Bible translators as a euphemism for 'penis.' It seems clear that sacred oaths between the Israelites were sealed by placing a hand on the male member. To swear on that mysterious organ was to swear to God ... Though few realize it, least of all in the courtroom, this idea of swearing a sacred oath by placing a hand under one's thigh (on or near the testicles) survives today – nearly four thousand years later – in the word 'testify'." – David M. Friedman, *A Mind of Its Own,* Penguin, New York, NY 2003, p. 114.

This meaning of the word "thigh" is confirmed by Strong in his definition of the Hebrew word #3409. He says that it is a euphemism for the "generative parts." (James Strong, *The Exhaustive Concordance of the Bible*). In addition to this word meaning "penis" being translated as "thigh," it is also translated "loins" (Genesis 46:26; Exodus 1:5) and "body" (Judges 8:30).

"Phallic oaths were sworn by grabbing or placing the hand on the genitals. This was a practice used ... by the Hebrews where it is witnessed through Abraham in Genesis 24:2-3, 9... More proof on the importance placed on 'genital oath' is found in Genesis 47:29." Robert W. Stace, *Why Weren't We Told?* 2001, pp. 70-71.

The Hebrew word for *"secrets"* here, according to *Strong's Hebrew Lexicon* (#4016), is *mâbûsh* for the *"the* (male) *pudenda."*

This verse surely demonstrates how nudism was common in Old Testament times.

> In ancient Egypt, poor men either wore a kilt and a girdle, or went naked while performing manual labor. While the Jews were slaves in Egypt, they probably followed the same custom. This made it possible for a woman coming to the rescue of her husband in a brawl to seize a man by his private parts, as we read in Deuteronomy 25:11.[5]

New Testament Examples

The Scriptures tell us that the Lord Jesus Christ laid aside His clothes during the "last supper" (John 13:4). Jesus appears not to be the only one, for afterwards Mark seems to be naked still (Mark 14:50-52).

Did you know that Peter fished in the nude (John 21:7)?

Paul was upon occasion found in a naked state in his ministry (I Corinthians 4:11; II Corinthians 11:27). Paul posed the question of whether nakedness could separate us from the love of Christ, to which he answers *"Nay, in all these things we are more than conquerors through Him Who loved us"* (Romans 8:35-37).

A Different View of Nudity

The Bible never describes human nakedness as *inherently* sinful. Except where forbidden in formal worship, or in cultural customs (examples: Exodus 20:26; 28:42-43; I Corinthians 11:5-6), there are *no* Biblical prohibitions of nakedness.[6]

Wherever shame is associated with nakedness in the Bible, it is a shame due to:

> Sinful conduct found in conjunction with nakedness (*examples:* Genesis 9:20-25; Jeremiah 13:26; Ezekiel 23:29-30; Habakkuk 2:15-16).

---

5. Otto A. Wall, *Sex and Sexual Worship,* College Park, MD. McGrath Publishing, 1970, p. 185. Cited by Tom Gruber, *What the Bible Really Says About Sex,* 2001, Trafford Publishing, p. 38.
6. We obviously exclude here the phrase *"uncover nakedness,"* which is a euphemism for sexual acts. In the context, this phrase is a reference to sinful sexual acts (see Leviticus 18:6-19; 20:11-21; *c.f.* Genesis 9:20-27).

Status of shame as a vanquished people deprived of their basic provisions (*examples:* Isaiah 20:4; Micah 1:11).

Figuratively, shame due to spiritual deficiency (*examples:* Revelation 3:17-18; 16:15).

The act of *clothing the naked* refers to the provision of *physical* needs, not *moral* needs (examples: Isaiah 58:7; Ezekiel 18:7, 16; Job 31:19; Matthew 25:36-43; James 2:15-16).

Though physical clothing (of various degrees) is regarded as a *moral* necessity in our "Victorian" and "Puritan" influenced society, such is not taught by the Bible. Have we ever considered the historical origins of the "Victorian" and "Puritan" attitude and standard?

By contrast, grace teaches the ineffectuality of external prohibitions based on human commands and teachings in controlling sinful desires (Colossians 2:20-23). Holy conduct is the result of the *internal* work of the Holy Spirit, not *external* rules and standards (Galatians 5:22-24).

Leviticus 18

One Bible passage sometimes raised as a prohibition of nudity is Leviticus 18. In this chapter, there are a number of kin whose *"nakedness"* should not be uncovered. One should not *"undress"* their father (:7), mother (:7), father's wife (:8), sister (:9, 11), granddaughter (:10), aunt (:12-13), uncle (:14), daughter-in-law (:15), or sister-in-law (:16).

If we were to take this issue of *"nudity"* literally, as some have absurdly tried to suggest, this would *not* forbid nudity in general, since there is absolutely nothing mentioned about the uncovering of the nudity of others, and of course anyone would obviously be allowed to undress themselves.

Thus, simple nudity is not the issue here. One would think that it should be so obvious to anyone reading the passage that the issue of "uncovering nakedness" is a figure of speech (euphemism) for sexual intercourse. The law was forbidding *incest* – sexual intercourse among those who are *"near of kin"* (:6).

An Historical Perspective of Nudity

GYMNASIUM

In 168 BC, a gym was built in Jerusalem where members engaged in nude sporting activities. "Gymnasium" is a Greek word that means "a place of nude exercise." Hebrews 4:13 says,

> *Neither is there any creature that is not manifest in his sight: but all things are naked and opened unto the eyes of Him with Whom we have to do.*

The Greek word for naked is *"gymnos"* [*Strong's Concordance*, Greek 1131].[7]

Public Baths

In the first centuries of Christianity, public baths – sometimes several acres in size – became a gathering place throughout the Roman Empire, similar to our shopping malls today. There were more than 850 public baths in Rome by the end of the fourth century. It is evident that Christians frequented these.[8]

Mixed nude bathing was customary for early Christians until about the end of the fourth century AD. Then the anti-body philosophy adopted by "the Church" took over. By the fifth century, Jerome considered it immoral for a Christian virgin to bathe in the nude – even if alone! This body-negative theology can be traced to Plato's negative view of the body, but it has absolutely nothing to do with the teachings of Jesus or the early Christians.

The YMCA

Swimming in the nude was common in American schools, at least by the boys. This also happened in the pools of the Christian YMCA. This stopped when mixed swimming was introduced, and nowadays the young Americans will hardly believe that their grandfathers swam nude.[9]

7. Gruber, *Op. Cit.*, p. 38.
8. Roy Bowen Ward, *Women in Roman Baths*, the Harvard Theological Review.
9. "Before the YMCA began to admit females in the early 1960's, swimming trunks were not even allowed in the pools, and high school swimming classes for boys sometimes had similar policies, citing the impracticality of providing and maintaining sanitary swimming gear. These practices were common because of the perception that there was nothing wrong or sexual about seeing members of the same gender in the nude, especially in these indoor contexts among equals in 'birthday suit uniform.'" – *Wikipedia Encyclopedia* (under "Skinny Dipping")

Chapter 5

Observations and Questions Related to Nudity and "Modesty"

The early days of my life as a believer were lived with an extremely legalistic attitude. My life was filled with many rules and regulations. I believed that my legalistic actions actually honored the Lord. I thought that outward form was the means to inward personal sanctification and the glorifying of the Lord.

As grace began to dawn upon my heart, again and again I was driven back to the Scriptures for a "fresh look." I continued to struggle with many issues, because my conscience was to some extent still under the sway of religion. I continued searching the Scriptures for answers to what seemed to me to be very tough questions. As I learned over the years, many of the issues on which I sought to find my scriptural bearings were really not moral issues at all, but religious and social ones. What I was coming to terms with were, in reality, just imposed religious and social scruples.

Our Purpose

The purpose of the observations and questions in this chapter is to bring to our thoughtful consideration some of the inconsistencies that may be present in our understanding of the particular subjects of nudity and "modesty."[1]

---

1. We will use the word *modest* in its various forms in quotation marks. We will do so because we believe it to be a misnomer in its currently used religious meaning. It is found only once in English Scripture *(King James Version)* and its meaning is *"of good behavior."* This can be seen by the fact that the Greek word used to translate *"modest"* in I Timothy 2:9 is also used once more, only a few verses away, in I Timothy 3:2, and is rendered *"of good behavior."*

Some of us probably believe that our views of these areas of life are solid and that they are based upon firm biblical standards. Nevertheless, I think that some basic examinations and inquiries of these areas may reflect, to some of us at least, a great inconsistency on our part. If so, we are hopeful that they will drive us back to the Scriptures for a fresh understanding of these subjects.

In the Beginning

> *And they were both naked, the man and his wife, and were not ashamed* (Genesis 2:25).

In the beginning God created Adam and Eve and left them naked in the garden of Eden. He called this nude condition *"good."*

> *And God saw every thing that He had made, and, behold, it was very good* ... (Genesis 1:31).

How long did God intend for them to be naked?

What place would clothing have had if the Eden fall had not taken place?

Why did Adam and Eve realize that they were naked after their fall? What had changed?

Was their reaction to the fall and their subsequent covering of themselves with fig leaves a result of their shame, or of their fear?

Why did God end up clothing Adam and Eve? What was the reason? Why did He not provide clothing for them before the fall, but did so after? What was the reason for the change? Would God's action be viewed as reactionary? Was He responding to their attempts to clothe themselves? Or did He have *another* purpose?

What was the divine purpose of clothing? Was it to conceal nudity – the state in which God had created them, having declared it to be *"good?"* Or was it primarily to protect the body from the effects of the curse?

Modesty: Absolute or Changing Standard?

Religious circles focus much on the subject of "modesty" especially when it comes to the issue of women.

"Modesty" is a key word with religionists as they quote I Timothy 2:9-10.

> *In like manner also, that women adorn themselves in* **modest** *apparel, with shamefacedness and sobriety; not with braided hair, or gold, or pearls, or costly array. But (which becomes women professing godliness) with good works.*

In accordance with their usage of this passage, what would be the normal amount of clothing that one should wear to be properly clothed, or to be "modest?"

Would this "modesty" be based upon an *absolute* scriptural standard from generation to generation, or would it be based upon *ever changing* social, cultural or religious standards?

Exactly what portions of the body would be clothed for one to be modest, and to what extent must they be covered? With what type of material must they be covered?

Does culture, society or religion play *any* role in this determination? (For example, there have been periods in our own national history when the exposure of the female wrist and ankles was viewed by some religionists as "immodest.")

"Proper" Clothing

What could, or should be defined as a "normal" amount of clothing? Is it *ever proper* for one to be less clothed than "normal?"

In what circumstances, if any, would it be proper to be less clothed than "normal?"

For example: Would one wearing a bathing suit be properly clothed? If so, under what circumstances? If it is appropriate to wear a bathing suit to the beach or pool, could one be worn to the grocery store, school, or to a religious service?

If it would be proper in one circumstance, but not in another, what would actually constitute the difference? Would it be an *absolute* moral standard? Or, would it be a *cultural* standard – that which is socially, or religiously acceptable?

If bathing suits are proper attire under certain circumstances, what would be the *practical* covering difference between bathing suits and underwear? Would it ever be proper to wear only underwear in public?

If a bathing suit is proper, which style? How much material should it have (in cubic inches) to be "modest?" Or, of what type of material would it be proper to make a bathing suit? Or, how much of the body can be exposed to view? What parts of the body is it proper to expose? What parts of the body is it not proper to expose?

What light, if any, do we gain from the actual Scripture in these areas? Or, are we left entirely to the direction of culture? As believers, is our view of "modest apparel" that which is only one generation, or one style behind the norm of the rest of our culture?

What standard is there, if there is any, of supposed "modest apparel?" Is that standard *absolute?*

What standard is there, if any, of proper circumstances for partial or full nudity? Is the standard different for different ages, or for different sexes?

What difference does age have to do with nudity? When is nudity proper for a baby, for example?

Is it ever proper for an infant to be nude? Under what circumstances would it be proper? For how long would it be appropriate?

When I was a child, as was a common practice, I was photographed in the nude. Was this appropriate? Would it be appropriate for me to be so photographed today? If so, under what conditions? If not, what would the difference be? Would the difference be an *absolute* moral standard? Or, would it be an *ever changing* cultural, social or religious one?

As an adult, is it ever proper to be nude or even partially nude? Again, what are the standards of these? What are the standards used to differentiate between full nudity and partial nudity?

For example, if I was to be seriously physically assaulted, would it be proper for a medical professional to photograph me in the nude as a record for future legal defense reasons?

As for the distinction of male and female, would it be "modest" and proper for a man to go topless? If so, under what circumstances? If there are any circumstances that it would be proper for a man to go topless (like at the beach, or at the pool), would it also be *moral* for a female to go topless in the same situations? What would the difference be?

Again for example, would it be proper to be nude or partially nude for the purpose of bathing? How about bathing in public, in the view of others, such as in a high school gym class, or at a local health club? Would this be proper? If so, by what standard? What if the class or club were coed? Would this be proper?

Further, would it ever be proper to disrobe for someone other than one's spouse? Would it be proper to disrobe for a medical professional, such as one's physician? If this would be *morally* acceptable, must this professional be of the same sex as their patient? For example, would it be proper for a female patient to be nude or partially nude with a male gynecologist? Or, would it be proper for a male patient to be nude or partially nude before a female urologist?

Would it be proper for a female nurse to bathe a disabled adult male, say in a hospital or nursing home? Would it be proper for a male nurse to bathe a disabled adult female?

What are the standards, if any, of acceptable "modesty" when it comes to being partially or fully naked? Would our standards be cultural, or Scriptural?

Would it ever be appropriate to have partial or full nudity in any other visual format, such as paintings, sculptures or photographs?

As for classic art work, there are many of the old masterpieces that have partial or full nudity. These include many religious renditions. Was it proper for the nude human form to be painted or sculpted? Was it appropriate for someone to model or pose in the nude for these? Is it "moral" or "modest" for them to be displayed and viewed? What standard would we use in making these determinations?

Is it ever appropriate for similar contemporary models to pose for a more modern form of art, such as photography? If so, under what circumstances? If not, and it was appropriate for the canvas and stone, what is the basis of the differing standard?

With the ever increasing technology of recent generations, would there ever be *any* circumstances in which it would be appropriate to photograph or video the partially nude, or fully nude human form?

How about in infants, such as myself as mentioned earlier? In 1959 I was not only photographed in the nude, but I was filmed receiving a bath from my parents and sister, with family friends watching and doing the filming. My sister was the central bather in this video record. Was it appropriate for my sister to be bathing me? Was it proper for family friends to be present? Was it acceptable for it to be recorded? What standards would we use to decide?

If that was acceptable, are there any other circumstances in which it might be appropriate for the filming of the nude human form?

When my wife and I were expecting our first child, we prepared by attending natural home birth classes. While attending such classes, we read materials that had birthing pictures for the purpose of education. Was it appropriate for us to view them? Was it proper for those in the photographs to allow themselves to be photographed naked, giving birth? Is it appropriate for such books to be written? Is it appropriate for them to be printed, published, and sold?

During these natural childbirth classes, we also attended a local community college and watched a film of an actual natural home birth. Was this morally wrong? Was it wrong of the husband and wife in the film to allow the graphic filming of the birth of their child? If so, why?

In fact, when my wife gave birth to our children, we took photographs of the birthing process. They obviously contained nudity. Was it wrong for me to do so? If not, for whom would it be appropriate for us to allow the viewing of these pictures, if anyone?

Was it wrong for me to take pictures of my wife in the nude? If the answer is no, could I do so again? If so, under what circumstances?

How about other educational nudity such as medical books?

Would it be appropriate for a medical student to study in detail – visually, through photographs, drawings, models, videos and "live" demonstrations – the body? If so, what would be the reasoning behind its appropriateness? Would such a study of the body be appropriate under any circumstances other than "medical?"

For example, would it be appropriate for a young husband (or an older one for that matter!) to view similar educational visual materials (photographs, drawings, videos, and live demonstrations, etc.) to learn the female body? Would it be acceptable for him to learn about his wife and how to care for her, and to please her physically and sexually by such means? Would it be appropriate for him to educate himself in such a way? If not, what would be the difference between his education and the education of an unmarried medical student? Why could a husband not be a student of the same materials?

For that matter, would it be appropriate for a man, in preparing for his wedding night, to educate himself in female anatomy and her sexual response? If not, why not? If so, would it be appropriate for him to use similar educational forms as the medical student? If not, why not?

How about nudity in other visual forms of media, such as magazines and movies? Under what circumstances would such ever be acceptable?

Consider the *National Geographic* magazine. Is it appropriate for this magazine to chronicle modern cultures where nudity is a fully acceptable standard? Is it appropriate for them to photograph these cultures and publish them? Is it appropriate for one to subscribe to them? If this is appropriate, why? If it is not proper, why not?

If it would be appropriate to view other cultures in a magazine such as *National Geographic*, could one *ever* view those of their own culture nude in a magazine? Why could one appropriately view the nudity of other cultures, but not their own? Has the *National Geographic* been a "moral" man's "appropriate" method of viewing the beauty of the human form?

If it is acceptable for *National Geographic* to publish such works, would it be equally acceptable for them (or other magazines) to chronicle the nude human form in our own modern subcultures? If not, why not?

Likewise, for video, is it appropriate for the *National Geographic Television*, the

Public Broadcasting System, the *Discovery Channel*, or *The Learning Channel*, for example, to air video chronicles of nudity from other modern cultures? Would it be proper for them to chronicle nudity from our own culture?

So, again, is nudity in art, photography or video *ever* acceptable, and if so under what circumstances? What are the guidelines? What is their source? Are these *guidelines* absolute, or *changing?*

How about advertisements of underwear and lingerie in newspapers and magazines, and specialty catalogs? Are such displays of the human body immoral? If so, why? If they are, should we support newspapers and magazines that display such advertising? Or should we support the clothing manufacturers who do such advertising?

The question at hand is simply this: What is "acceptable" nudity? Moreover, who sets the standard of what acceptable nudity is? Furthermore, is this standard *absolute,* or *changing?*

The Factor of Fashion in Relationship to Nudity

One author considers the area of clothing and fashion.

> The history of **clothing** and **fashion,** which **is** so closely associated therewith, affords us the most important elements for the understanding of the sense of shame of modern man, and for the judgment of its importance and of its natural limitations. [Emphasis is the author's]
>
> Clothing through the intermediation of fashion … has led astray the natural biological sense of shame, since it is the sole cause of the "exaggerated sense of shame" known as **prudery.** Prudery recognizes the existence of **clothed** human beings only; it will not recognize the existence of naked man; it refuses to admit the purely moral-aesthetic influence of natural nudity – to prudery this is something immoral and repulsive.
>
> To prudery alone we must ascribe the fact that we modern civilized human beings have completely lost the taste for natural nudity, and also for the natural sense of shame, and thus we show little understanding of the ennobling, civilizing influence of both …

At the present day the natural justifiable sense of shame has been **intensified** to an unnatural degree, and has been falsified to such an extent that this exaggeration of the sense of shame, the unceasing objective suppression of natural harmless activities and feelings, has really increased the hidden desires to an immeasurable degree; it is this, in fact, which heaps fuel on the fire of fleshly lust.[2]

Can one *ever* be fully or partially nude? What circumstances would allow for varying degrees of nudity? For whom would it be appropriate to view someone naked? What, if any thing, does age, sex, circumstances, and culture have to do with nudity?

What passages of Scripture provide guidance to you in these areas? Do you know of any?

What about the "modesty" passage in I Timothy chapter 2? Again, we shall look at that and other related Bible texts in the next chapter.

Our purpose in this particular chapter is not to suggest that we return to a Victorian, Puritan standard of dress, nor is it to suggest that we walk around in the nude. The purpose is for us to evaluate seriously *our* "standards," and to ascertain their true origin. Is our understanding of nudity Scriptural, or is it social and religious?

---

2. Iwan Bloch, *The Sexual Life of Our Time: In Its Relations to Modern Civilization*, Allied Book Company, n.d., pp. 133, 155, 157.

Chapter 6

Modest Apparel

A Commentary on I Timothy 2:9-10

In like manner also, that women adorn themselves in modest apparel, with shamefacedness and sobriety; not with braided hair, or gold, or pearls, or costly array; but (which becomes women professing godliness) with good works (I Timothy 2:9-10).

In this chapter we shall take a look at the first of two passages of Scripture (I Timothy 2:9-10 and I Peter 3:3-6) that often are used to bring people under the bondage of an unbiblical standard of supposed *"modest apparel."* As we clearly shall see, these passages have to do with the heart, rather than *"the outward appearance."*

Paul and Peter are but echoing and expounding upon an important principle that is rooted in the Old Testament.

For the LORD sees not as man sees; for man looks on the outward appearance, but the LORD looks on the heart (I Samuel 16:7).

I Timothy 2:9-10

Adorn

The word *"adorn"* is *Strong's Greek Lexicon* #2885, *kosmeo*, meaning "to put in proper order."

It should be apparent to the careful observer of the Word of God that Paul uses this word *"adorn"* here in a spiritual sense. He is not referring to material clothing; for he clearly writes *"not with …"* He is making a contrast between physical clothing and spiritual clothing. Paul also speaks of spiritual apparel in Titus 2:9-10.

> *Exhort servants to be obedient unto their own masters, and to please them well in all things; not answering again; not purloining, but showing all good fidelity; that they may **adorn the doctrine** of God our Savior in all things.*

One should also compare this with Paul's *"put on"* passages:

> *The night is far spent, the day is at hand: let us therefore cast off the works of darkness, and let us **put on** the armor of light. Let us walk honestly, as in the day; not in rioting and drunkenness, not in chambering and wantonness, not in strife and envying. But **put on** the Lord Jesus Christ, and make not provision for the flesh, to fulfill the lusts thereof* (Romans 13:12-14).

> *For as many of you as have been baptized into Christ have **put on** Christ* (Galatians 3:27).

> *And that you **put on** the new man, which after God is created in righteousness and true holiness. … **Put on** the whole armor of God, that you may be able to stand against the wiles of the devil* (Ephesians 4:24; 6:11).

> *And have **put on** the new man, which is renewed in knowledge after the image of Him Who created him … **Put on** therefore, as the elect of God, holy and beloved, bowels of mercies, kindness, humbleness of mind, meekness, longsuffering; forbearing one another, and forgiving one another, if any man has a quarrel against any: even as Christ forgave you, so also do you. And above all these things **put on** charity, which is the bond of perfectness* (Colossians 3:10-14).

Modest

The word *"modest"* is Strong's *Greek Lexicon #2887, kosmios,* meaning "orderly."

THE *DEFINITION* OF OUR ENGLISH WORD "MODEST"

> That lowly temper which accompanies a moderate estimate of one's own worth and importance. … Humble, unobtrusive deportment, as opposed to extreme boldness, forwardness, arrogance, presumption, audacity or impudence." – Noah Webster, *American Dictionary of the English Language.*

THE *ETYMOLOGY* OF OUR ENGLISH WORD "MODEST"

> "1531, moderation," Robert K. Barnhart, *The Barnhart Concise Dictionary of Etymology*; Moderate meaning, "not excessive or extreme, not extravagant." – Noah Webster, *American Dictionary of the English Language;*
>
> Not excessive. – T.F. Hoad, *Oxford Concise Dictionary of English Etymology.*

This Greek word (*kosmios*) is only used twice in the Bible. The only other place this word is used is just a few verses away, and it is then translated in the *King James Version* as *"of good behavior."*

> *A bishop then must be blameless, the husband of one wife, vigilant, sober, **of good behavior,** given to hospitality, apt to teach* (I Timothy 3:2).

One should also note our English word *behavior* in the context of Titus 2:3-5.

> *The aged women likewise, that they be in **behavior** as becomes holiness, not false accusers, not given to much wine, teachers of good things; That they may teach the young women to be sober, to love their husbands, to love their children, To be discrete, chaste, keepers at home, good, obedient to their own husbands, that the Word of God be not blasphemed."*

Another English word with the same etymological roots is *moderation*. Paul writes,

> *Let your **moderation** be known unto all men* ... (Philippians 4:5).

Moderation is *Strong's Greek Lexicon* #1933, *epieikes*, meaning "appropriate, i.e., (by implication) mild," and is also translated as *"gentle"* and *"patient"* in the *King James Version.*

Apparel

The word *"apparel"* is *Strong's Greek Lexicon* #2689, *katastole*, meaning "costume."

This is the only place where this Greek word is used. Its root word *katastello* (#2687) may give us better insight into its meaning. This root word is translated in the *King James Version* as *"quiet"* in Acts 19:36.

Seeing then that these things cannot be spoken against, you ought to be **quiet,** *and to do nothing rashly.*

It is then obvious to the student of Scripture that, when Paul speaks of *"modest apparel,"* he is actually talking about *"quiet behavior."* Interestingly enough, the word that appears between these two words in *Strong's Greek Lexicon* is *katastema* (#2688), and has the meaning of *"demeanor."* It is translated *"behavior"* in Titus 2:3.

The aged women likewise, that they be in **behavior** *as becomes holiness ...*

Shamefacedness

The word *shamefacedness* is *Strong's Greek Lexicon* #127, *aidos,* meaning "... reverence, awe, respect ..." – George W. Knight, III, *Commentary on the Pastoral Epistles*, Grand Rapids, MI, W.B. Eerdmans Publishing Company, 1992, p. 134.

The King James Version translates this word as *"reverence"* in Hebrews 12:28.

Wherefore we receiving a kingdom which cannot be moved, let us have grace, whereby we may serve God acceptably with **reverence** *and godly fear.*

Compare this with Ephesians 5:33:

Nevertheless let every one of you in particular so love his wife even as himself; and the wife see that she **reverence** *her husband.*

Sobriety

The word *sobriety* is *Strong's Greek Lexicon* #4997, *sophrosune,* meaning "soundness of mind ... self-control."

Not ... but

Paul is saying, "I'm *not* talking about this, *but* I'm talking about that."

But *... with good works.*

The issue here clearly is the adornment of heart subjection by the wife to her husband, as is the case in the parallel passage of I Peter 3, which we will look at in our next chapter.

Chapter 7

Modest Apparel
A Commentary on 1 Peter 3:3-6

Whose adorning let it not be that outward adorning of plaiting [braiding] the hair, and of wearing of gold, or of putting on of apparel; but let it be the hidden man of the heart, in that which is not corruptible, even the ornament of a meek and quiet spirit, which is in the sight of God of great price. For after this manner in the old time the holy women also, who trusted in God, adorned themselves, being in subjection unto their own husbands: even as Sara obeyed Abraham, calling him lord: whose daughters you are, as long as you do well, and are not afraid with any amazement (I Peter 3:3-6).

In this chapter we will take a brief look at the parallel passage to I Timothy 2:9-10.

Adorning

The word *"adorning"* is *Strong's Greek Lexicon* #2889, *kosmos*, meaning "orderly arrangement."

Outward

The word *"outward"* is *Strong's Greek Lexicon* #1855, *exothen*, meaning "external(-ly)."

Hidden

The word *"hidden"* is *Strong's Greek Lexicon #2927, kruptos,* meaning "concealed."

Meek

The word *"meek"* is *Strong's Greek Lexicon #4239, praus,* meaning "mild … humble."

Quiet

The word *"quiet"* is *Strong's Greek Lexicon #2272, hesuchios.*

Adorned

The word *"adorned"* is *Strong's Greek Lexicon #2885* (See notes on I Timothy 2 in the last article).

Subjection

The word *"subjection"* is *Strong's Greek Lexicon #5293, hupotasso,* meaning "to subordinate … to obey."

Obeyed

The word *"obeyed"* is *Strong's Greek Lexicon #5219, hupakouo,* meaning "to listen attentively … to heed or conform to a command or authority."

Lord

The word *"lord"* is *Strong's Greek Lexicon #2962, kurios,* meaning "supreme in authority."

Not

Again, the *"Not … But."* Peter, too, is saying, "I'm *not* talking about this, *but* I'm talking about that."

Outward

Peter says,

> Let it **NOT** be that outward adorning … **BUT** let it be the hidden man of the heart.

The outward is where religion focuses. Both Peter and Paul are saying that this is **NOT** where our focus is.

> For man looks on the outward appearance, but the LORD looks on the heart (I Samuel 16:7).

> Woe unto you, scribes and Pharisees, hypocrites! for you are like unto whited sepulchres, which indeed **appear beautiful outwardly,** but are within full of dead men's bones, and of all uncleanness (Matthew 23:27).

> For which cause we faint not; but though our **outward** man perishes, yet the inward man is renewed day by day (II Corinthians 4:16).

> Do you look on things after the **outward appearance?** If any man trusts to himself that he is Christ's, let him of himself think this again, that, as he is Christ's, even so are we Christ's (II Corinthians 10:7).

Hidden

This word is translated as *"inwardly"* in Romans 2:29 in the *King James Version*.

> But he is a Jew, who is one **inwardly;** and circumcision is that of the heart, in the spirit, and not in the letter; whose praise is not of men, but of God.

Lord

This word is translated as *"sir(s)"* ten times in the *King James Version*, and is a term of respect and reverence.

Neither the style, length nor cut of clothing is the intent of these passages. Neither is it the wearing of different jewelry, nor particular hair styles. God's intention is that the woman relates to her husband in meekness, sobriety and reverence. This is the same manner that the husband should exhibit in our relationship with the Lord.

Chapter 8

Lust in the Bible

You shall not covet your neighbor's house, you shall not covet your neighbor's wife, nor his manservant, nor his maidservant, nor his ox, nor his ass, nor any thing that is your neighbor's (Exodus 20:17).

The word *"covet"* in this verse is the Hebrew word *"châmad."* It is Strong's *Hebrew Lexicon* #2530, and is there defined, "to delight in." It is also translated elsewhere in the *King James Version* as *"delight," "desire,"* and *"lust."*

All three of these words can be used in a good sense, or in a bad sense. As with other words, it is the context that helps to determine the usage.

There are good and evil lusts. Both types can be found throughout the Scriptures.

EVIL LUSTS

An example of evil lust can be seen in our text. It was clearly wrong to desire for one's own anything that belonged to one's neighbor – whether it was his home, his wife, his servants, or even his livestock. These all rightfully belonged to one's neighbor.

Another passage of notable interest is Habakkuk 2:9.

Woe to him who covets an evil covetousness to his house …

Notice that the context here is specifically regarding one who covets an *"evil covetousness."*

The word covetousness here is the Hebrew word *betsa'. Strong's Hebrew Lexicon* #1215 defines it as "plunder," and in the *King James Version* it is translated as *"dishonest gain"* in Ezekiel 22:13, 27.

Thus, evil covetousness is the inordinate desiring of that which rightfully belongs to another (*c.f.* our text – Exodus 20:17). Evil covetousness is the inordinate *desire* to take away for one's own that which rightfully belongs to another. While theft is the *act of taking* that which rightfully belongs to another, covetousness is the *desire* to do so (whether the desire is acted upon or not.)

Here are two excellent examples of the nature of evil covetousness that is manifested in action:

> *And they covet fields, and take them by violence; and houses, and take them away: so they oppress a man and his house, even a man and his heritage* (Micah 2:2).

> *When I saw among the spoils a goodly Babylonish garment, and two hundred shekels of silver, and a wedge of gold of fifty shekels weight, then I coveted them, and took them; and, behold, they are hidden in the earth in the midst of my tent, and the silver under it* (Joshua 7:21).

The answer to evil lust (covetousness) is found in simply loving one's neighbor. This will cause us not to defraud them of what rightfully belongs to them, whether it is in heart alone (covetousness), or in heart as well as actions (theft).

> *For this, "You shall not commit adultery, You shall not kill, You shall not steal, You shall not bear false witness, You shall not covet;" and if there is any other commandment, it is briefly comprehended in this saying, namely, "You shall love your neighbor as yourself." Love works no ill to his neighbor: therefore love is the fulfilling of the law* (Romans 13:9-10).

GOOD LUSTS

Now we will take a look at good lust. Examples of good lust can be found in the following Scripture passages:

> *But **covet** earnestly the best gifts: and yet show I unto you a more excellent way* (I Corinthians 12:31).

*Wherefore, brothers, **covet** to prophesy, and forbid not to speak with tongues* (I Corinthians 14:39).

*For the flesh **lusts** against the Spirit, and the Spirit against the flesh: and these are contrary the one to the other: so that you cannot do the things that you would* (Galatians 5:17).

*The **desire** of the righteous is only good: but the expectation of the wicked is wrath* (Proverbs 11:23).

*For I am in a strait between two, having a **desire** to depart, and to be with Christ; which is far better* (Philippians 1:23).

*But we, brothers, being taken from you for a short time in presence, not in heart, endeavoured the more abundantly to see your face with great **desire*** (I Thessalonians 2:17).

*This is a true saying, "If a man **desires** the office of a bishop, he **desires** a good work"* (I Timothy 3:1).

As can be seen clearly from these passages of Scripture, there can be good lusts (desires) as well as evil ones.

Now applying this word to our subject at hand we should be able to come to a clear understanding that sexual desire, or sexual lust can be good or evil. In and of itself, sexual desire is in *no way* evil. Loving sexual lust is in fact normal and healthy. It is a part of God's grand design for man. Sexual desire has been firmly planted within the heart of mankind.

Man has the ability to experience sexual needs, desires, excitement, and passion because of the way God has designed him. It is a part of humanity's core makeup. It is only good or evil based upon what is done with it. Moreover, the way all this works itself out in the life of a believer may be far different than you think. We will explore these truths more clearly in our next few chapters.

Chapter 9

Morality:
Social and Religious Folkways

One would think, listening to the teachers of religion, moral crusaders, and the political right-wing pundits of our day that the words *moral, morality, immoral* and *immorality* would surely be spread extensively across the pages of the Holy Scriptures. One would probably be shocked to find out that they do not appear, not even *once*.

It is amazing how words such as these have worked themselves into the framework of Christendom. Morals have *nothing* to do with the Scriptures themselves. What they have to do with is the customs of one's particular social culture. For *"custom"* is the actual meaning of this word *moral*. Thus, instead of an absolute standard, like the Scriptures, morals are based upon the customs of ever changing and varied cultures within societies.

ETYMOLOGY

Latin *mos* "custom" is the starting point of the English family of "morality" words.[1]

Latin *moralis*, from *mos* "custom."[2]

---

1. John Ayto, *Dictionary of Word Origins.*
2. *Oxford Concise Dictionary,* Oxford University Press.

L. *moralis,* from *mos, moris,* manner.[3]

a manner, custom.[4]

manner, custom.[5]

customs, manners.[6]

ethical folkways.[7]

Merriam-Webster states that, "Moral implies conformity to *established sanctioned codes* or *accepted notions* of right and wrong (the basic *moral* values of a *community*)."

In spite of the fact that the "moral" family of words do not appear in the Bible, a society's system of morality is often made equal to the Scripture. One can hear the religious moralist, "A good Christian would never _____" – and the blank would be filled in by a currently accepted traditional religious moral taboo.

The fact is, religion loves and incubates things like the *"Moral Majority,"* i.e., customs based upon popular consensus (the so-called "majority"). Religious legalism adores dominating others by pressing its version of "morality" upon the masses! They are moral lords over the people. This is the oppressive heart of Roman Catholicism, and it is alive and "well" in Roman Protestantism.

MORALITY AND MODESTY
IN DIFFERENT SOCIETIES

Consider Ralph Woodrow's comments regarding the moral view of modesty from his wonderful work, *Women's Adornment.*

> Ideas about "modesty" have varied greatly in different countries. In old China, exposure of the upper-class women's tiny feet was regarded as most indecent. Such were considered the most sexually stimulating parts of the body. Virgin goddesses were sometimes portrayed with shoes, even when otherwise stark

---

3. Noah Webster, An *American Dictionary of the English Language,* 1828.
4. Walter W. Skeat, *The Concise Dictionary of English Etymology.*
5. Ernest Weekly, *An Etymological Dictionary of Modern English.*
6. Robert K. Barnhart, *The Barnhart Concise Dictionary of Etymology.*
7. Eric Partridge, *Origins: A Short Etymological Dictionary of Modern English.*

naked. In early Japan, a woman's eyebrows were considered as among her greatest charms. Some husbands would shave their brides' eyebrows off in an attempt to make them unattractive to other men. Among some people, a woman's hair was considered a sexual stimulant – that the mere sight of her hair aroused a man's passions. Thus it had to be covered.[8]

Robertson McQuilkin makes a similar point.

> That which is tempting differs from society to society and from era to era. In India, for example, the calves of a woman's legs are covered, but not necessarily the midriff. In old Japan it was the nape of the neck that enticed, and the daring geisha would arrange the collar of her kimono to expose a bit more of her neck. In certain African tribes the loose woman wears a bra and the modest girl goes topless, whereas in a South American tribe it is the opposite: modest women wear sleeves and tops, but no bottoms. The most shameful thing would be to expose the armpits. Modesty, then, has something to do with culture – how dress is viewed by a particular people.[9]

C.S. Lewis wisely observed,

> A girl in the Pacific islands wearing hardly any clothes and a Victorian lady completely covered in clothes might both be equally "modest," proper, or decent, according to the standards of their own societies: and both, for all we could tell by their dress, might be equally chaste (or equally unchaste).[10]

THE VICTORIAN MORALS

Richard Lewinsohn, speaking of Victorian morals, states,

> In the Victorian Age ladies had no legs. Anything which might suggest that women might have nether limbs, even for the purpose of walking, was regarded as objectionable. Even the thought of the anatomy of the lower half of a woman's body was "shocking." Below the waist there existed nothing but a skirt, or rather a whole array of skirts so starched that they could stand up against the strongest wind.[11]

---

8. Ralph Woodrow, *Women's Adornment.*
9. Robertson McQuilkin, *An Introduction To Biblical Ethics,* Tyndale House Publishers, 1989, p. 231.
10. C.S. Lewis, *Mere Christianity,* Book III Christian Behavior, chapter 5.
11. Richard Lewinsohn, *A History of Sexual Customs,* translated by Alexander Mayce, Harper & Brothers, 1958, p. 293.

Others, addressing the same issue of Victorian morals, have written similarly.

It was a logical development of this unnatural and artificially induced horror of anything associated, however remotely, with sexual or evacuatory activities, that led to the Victorian concealment of even the legs of their pianos.[12]

Prudery was the order of the [Victorian] day. ... Books were strictly censored ... Words such as "womb" and "belly" were, in some cases, expurgated from the Bible and prayerbook. ... "Leg" was a word not to be used by any decent woman; thus one had to speak of the "limbs" of the table or piano. The "limbs" of some furniture were covered by skirts because some women wanted to avoid any appearance of nudity! ... Some newspapers felt it was too delicate to mention the birth of a child ...[13]

During the Victorian era, "cages were manufactured which were fitted over a boy's genitals at night and carefully locked; some, for better protection, had spikes sticking out of them."[14]

Another consequence of prudery was the lack of sexual hygiene. ... Regular washing of the genitals might induce impure thoughts in a girl and lead to masturbation, if to nothing worse. That alone was enough to ban it from any Victorian home.[15]

After all, the "Early Church Father" Jerome (340-420) condemned virgins bathing.

Speaking personally, I altogether disapprove of baths for a full-grown virgin. She ought to blush and be unable to behold her own nakedness.[16]

[Peter] Lombard, however, argues that the Holy Spirit absents himself even from the room of married folk performing the act only for purposes of generation.[17]

Under Victoria, divorce could not be mentioned at Court. Divorced husbands

12. Frank Bottomley, *Attitudes To The Body In Western Christendom,* Lepus Books, 1979, p. 146.
13. Letha Scanzoni, *Sex and the Single Eye,* Zondervan, 1968, p. 37.
14. Lewinsohn,*Op. Cit.,* p. 294.
15. *Ibid.*
16. Jerome, *Select Letters,* Loeb, 1966, cvii, 11, cited by Frank Bottomley, *Attitudes To The Body In Western Christendom,* Lepus Books, 1979, pp. 77-78.
17. Raymond J. Lawrence, Jr., *The Poisoning of Eros: Sexual Values in Conflict,* Augustine Moore Press, 1989, p. 30.

or wives were not admitted to Buckingham Palace. Even foreign Powers had to submit to this rule: no diplomat who had been divorced was accredited to the court of St. James.[18]

18th and 19th century Roman Catholic moralists continued with the fascination they inherited from the medieval church with its vivid details of all aspects of sexual behavior, especially including the so-called "solitary sins." So, for example, the Jesuits went so far as to invent a stick to be used in dressing that would permit a cleric to tuck in his shirt while guarding against inadvertently touching his genitals. The Jesuit saint, Aloyisha Gonzaga (1568-1591), is said never to have looked even his mother in the face so as to avoid sexual temptation.[19]

[T]he twentieth century J.B. Phillips translation of the New Testament quite tellingly translates the "kiss" as "handshake."[20]

OUR OWN SOCIETY

One can easily track the change of moral folkways in our own society by looking back over the past century. To some, uncovered female ankles were considered quite immoral. So was the public usage of the word "pregnant." Moreover, here was an age in which married couples were shown on television to sleep in separate twin beds. Examples of that age are "I Love Lucy" and "The Dick Van Dyke Show."

TWO EXTREME VIEWS OF SEXUALITY

Earl Paulk, in his work *Sex Is God's Idea,* develops for us the two basic extremes regarding our society's views of sexuality.

The Playboy Philosophy

The "playboy" philosophy of human sexuality disregards the fact that God created sex and called it "good." This philosophy flaunts sexuality at the Church like naughty children who willfully insist on disobeying the rules at school. Unfortunately, the Church too often has played the role of a strict schoolmaster in this moral scenario – frowning on all suggestions that sex is indeed a very beautiful, pleasurable, acceptable means of communication between a man and a woman.

---

18. Lewinsohn, *Op. Cit.* p. 289.
19. Lawrence, Jr., *Op. Cit.* pp. 201-202.
20. *Ibid*, p. 85.

The Victorian Philosophy

The other extreme in social, sexual values is an oppressive "Victorian" regard for sexuality in which people try to hide a normal experience of human life which is undeniably obvious. An oppressive view of sexuality undermines any healthy view of the subject by implying that sexual intimacy is necessary to produce children, but any other reason is sinful, risqué and taboo. Too many Christians live their entire lives in emotional bondage which produce guilt. Unfortunately, the Church has traditionally commended suppression because it maintains behavior codes which appear to be "spiritual."

As a young pastor who was called into the ministry at the age of seventeen, I can remember a pastor saying to me, "If you ever touch a woman, your ministry is over!" I lived years of my life in complete adherence to a rigid morality which was devoid of any expressions of compassion or tenderness. Fear ruled my emotions. My pharisaic morals caused me to be a strict disciplinarian and a harsh judge of others who would "fall into sin." Inside an emotional prison, I was so threatened by the possibility of "wrong" feelings that even proper, approved relationships were strained at times under tremendous convictions that I must "deny the flesh."

My impeccable moral standards were controlled by the expectations of the Church and society. Only years later through a series of devastating circumstances did I begin to comprehend that God's desires in Christian relationships are demonstrated in the example of Jesus Christ. Jesus loved people with a freedom and purity that accepted them wherever they were in their lives and lifted them to a higher, purer realm. He loved women as well as other men. He was touchable and physically expressive. He had no fear of being close to people and allowed them to express their affections to Him openly in spite of criticism from "religious" leaders.

Jesus deliberately broke moral codes of His day to love and minister to certain people. He probably even confused His disciples with His conversation with the Samaritan woman at the well who was "living with" her latest (at least number six) boyfriend (John 4). His virtue healed a woman with an issue of blood when the Mosaic law forbade a man to touch her (Mark 5:25-30). His disciples were certainly not the type of men the Church would normally ordain as pastors: unscrupulous businessmen (Matthew 21:31) and burly fishermen with crude language and unrefined manners …

The Pharisees behaved as if normal human needs never existed. The Pharisees never admitted to having ... normal feelings ... Physical desires are an important part of man as God created him. Until we understand and acknowledge this area of man's nature, we will never be able to move to the higher spiritual dimensions that God has given us the capacity to enjoy. Paul said, *"That was not first which is spiritual, but that which is natural; and afterward that which is spiritual"* (I Corinthians 15:46). Paul asks, *"Doth not even nature itself teach you ...?"* (I Corinthians 11:14).

Sex is God's idea. Christian sexuality is as much a demonstration of God's goodness and love as giving to the poor or sharing the plan of salvation with someone. Christian sexual intimacy is a witness to the world of love relationships which are given and blessed by God ... God is searching for people who are boldly challenging every worldly distortion of His goodness and love.[21]

RELIGIOUS MORALITY

Listen to another former pastor,

Biblical sexual "morality" does not even *resemble* modern "Christian" sexual "morality"... Nothing is sinful because "it just seems to be wrong." Subjective opinions, even if followed by the masses, can never establish a thing as sinful; otherwise sin becomes whatever people think sin to be. Sin is *only* what God *says* it is ... Preachers, pastors, church leaders in general, learn their concepts from their peers just like all men do. Few of them are willing to expend the time and energy required of examining, *for themselves,* every line of biblical text. It is just too easy to take for granted what passes muster in the majority of churches, as being the "biblical norm."

As an ex-pastor I can say from experience that it is unusual to find preachers who do their own study. Most of them are pressed for time and know too little about using Bible study tools. Copying their messages from another's material is a standard solution for many Christian teachers. Thus in many areas, what is preached *is* merely what *has been* preached, and only occasionally does it meet the test of true biblical scholarship.

What rules the day as "biblical morality" is not truly *biblical* at all. It is *religious morality* ... Modern religious sexual standards have been developed over time

21. Earl Paulk, *Sex Is God's Idea,* K Dimension Publishers, 1985, pp. 5-7, 26, 34.

by the human penchant for filling in the gaps left by God's silence on most sexual topics.

That these human standards have become almost universally accepted in the church does not make them other than human standards. They still lack God's authority. The Bible still does not teach them despite the many who believe otherwise... The modern Christian church is a self-appointed, worldwide enforcer of a multitude of heavy sexual burdens that it has *"laid upon men's shoulders"* (Matthew 23:4), threatening people everywhere ... Millions of people are afraid of sex, confused about sex and "guilty" about sex, all because of the faulty standards set by an apostate church.

Sex has become the unmentionable subject, and a "nasty" practice because of the church's ignorance ... Where God has granted liberty the church has denied it. What God has not seen fit even to *comment* on, the church has boldly and adamantly *legislated* ...

Only after understanding what God says about sex in the Bible, will any person be able to form a right opinion about it. And it is useless to answer with, "But there are some things that are just *obviously* wrong." ... What is obviously wrong to one group of people is just as obviously right to another group of people. Our subjective opinions, regardless of how deeply we feel them, can never be made the basis for moral standards. Our obligation is simple.

Let God be God! Let God do all the legislating about all sexual matters ... Religious leaders have much to gain by not questioning the status quo and many will not even seriously consider any alternate viewpoint in any sexual matter. They have been trained by their mentors, pressured by their peers, and threatened by their financial insecurity to give nothing but the majority report on sexual issues. So if you want to be confident that you are getting close to objective Bible truth, *look for yourself.* You will be amazed, even flabbergasted at what you find when you look for yourself, with eyes that want to see what is in the Bible. You may even be angry at what has been kept from you by those who were responsible to tell you, "just the truth ma'am," but who, for many reasons, could not find the truth for themselves.[22]

---

22. Philo Thelos, *Divine Sex: Liberating Sex from Religious Tradition* (2002), pp. i, iv, xii, xiii, xv, 139, 155.

Chapter 10

Adultery in the Bible

In the Bible adultery has to do with *betrayal*. It has to do with the taking of something that rightfully belongs to another. Adultery is therefore associated in the Scriptures with theft and deceit. It is the working of ill against one's neighbor, to defraud him of what is duly his (Romans 13:10). It may best be defined by our modern usage of the word "cheating."

Adultery is a sin committed *with* (or by) another man's wife (Leviticus 20:10; *c.f.* Proverbs 6:29; Jeremiah 29:23). Adultery is a sin against possession.[1] It is committed *against* the husband. Because it is a sin associated with possession, it is often found in the same context with stealing (Exodus 20:14-15; Deuteronomy 5:18-19; Job 24:14-15).[2]

The Hebrew word for adultery has the figurative meaning "to apostatize" (*Strong's Hebrew Lexicon #5003*), conveying the idea of a forsaking.

Webster shows that the English word "apostasy" has an etymology meaning "to depart." He offers these words in his definition:

abandonment ... desertion ... or departure.

---

1. "The crime of adultery would be an offense against your property – a theft if the woman is older, and theft with property damage if the woman is a virgin." T.J. Hornsby, *Sex Texts from the Bible*, p. 30.
2. The married woman participating in this sin against possession is called an "adulteress" – *"And the man who commits adultery with another man's wife, even he who commits adultery with his neighbor's wife, the adulterer and the adulteress shall surely be put to death"* (Leviticus 20:10, c.f. Proverbs 6:26; Hosea 3:1; Romans 7:3).

Thus, adultery is a forsaking of one's husband, being unfaithful to the bond – a betrayal, a "cheating"[3] on them. The virtue at issue is that of honesty, faithfulness, commitment and TRUST – being **true** (being *un*adulterated).

The commandment *"thou shalt not commit adultery,"* might be understood as "thou shalt not betray." The issue of adultery is *not* primarily sexual: it is the sin of betrayal – in the sexual arena. The commandment does not say who should not commit betrayal, nor against whom. Understood in its most general application, it could be applied to *any* relationship, thus, "thou shalt not betray … thy Lord, thy wife, thy husband, thy children, thy parents, thy friends, thy neighbors, etc."

Again, this is an issue of trust. It is a commandment against betrayal, against being a Judas, or a Benedict Arnold – a traitor! It is used, in its spiritual context, of Israel against the Lord.

Adultery in its sexual context is an illegitimate relation with or by another man's wife. It is a sin against the ownership of the husband over his wife.[4] Therefore, adultery is *primarily* a sin against the husband and not against God.[5]

The wife is under the authority of her husband. In the Bible married men would have sex with multiple wives, concubines, servants, handmaidens and non-cultic prostitutes, none of which was called adultery, because it did not violate the "possession" of a husband.

Consider the following comments quoted from a well known and respected Bible dictionary:

> He [the husband] might have more wives than one, or have intercourse with a person not espoused or married to him, without being considered an adulterer …[6]

---

3. "The act of defrauding by deceitful arts." Noah Webster, *American Dictionary of the English Language,* 1828.

4. Not all "non-husband and non-wife" sexual relations in the Bible were viewed as sinful. Sexual relations with permission, that did not involve betrayal, were not classified as adultery. This principle can be clearly seen in Numbers 5:12-13. Note the added phrase, *"and it be hid from the eyes of her husband."* (Review *The Sexual Needs of Servants,* in the section on "Commonness of Sexuality" in the Bible" in chapter 2). Samson, a man of faith and righteousness (Hebrews 11:32-33), gives his wife to his friend (Judges 14:20). It is simply and undramatically stated without any divine reproof.

5. The biblical issue of the sin against the husband primarily related to the purity of his bloodline. Sexual intercourse of a wife outside of marriage would cause an unsure or unclean bloodline or birth line. Genealogies were of the utmost importance in the Old Testament.

6. *Unger's Bible Dictionary,* Moody Press.

Another recognized source states,

> A man was not considered an adulterer if he engaged in sexual relations
> with a female slave (Genesis 16:1-4), a prostitute (Genesis 38:15-18), or his
> wife's handmaid with the spouse's permission (Genesis 16:4). Nor was a man
> deemed to be in an adulterous relationship if he happened to be married to
> two wives.[7]

According to *Harper's Bible Commentary,* adultery in the Old Testament,

> did not correspond to our notions of the act.[8]

Still another biblical reference resource declares,

> To the husband was granted much more liberty. Although he also was
> forbidden to commit adultery with another man's wife, he was allowed to
> increase the number of his own wives and concubines, according to his
> desires and means, and also to have intercourse with women outside of his
> own house, provided only that these were not already bound by betrothal or
> by a completed marriage. In case he violated a still free virgin, he was dealt
> with according to the law in Exodus 22:15; Deuteronomy 22:28f. What a wife
> was entitled to demand from a husband is told in Exodus 21:10. We nowhere
> read anything to the effect that he was forbidden extramarital intercourse with
> other women.[9]

Most modern Christians are ignorant of the biblical framework of sexuality, so as
not to have the frame of reference to fully understand the issue of adultery.

To assist us in a clearer historical and Biblical perspective, Raymond Lawrence
writes,[10]

> The Old Testament texts began to be read in the church through the lens of
> Platonism. The popular modern understanding of the Torah's commandment
> against adultery represents one of those platonically biased misreadings of
> ancient tradition ... Since a woman was regarded normally as attached to

---

7. *Baker's Evangelical Dictionary of Biblical Theology,* Immorality, Sexual.
8. *Harper's Bible Commentary,* (cited by Tom Gruber, *What the Bible Really Says About Sex,* 2001, Trafford Publishing, p. 10).
9. *A New Standard Bible Dictionary* (Marriage and Divorce), Funk & Wagnalls, 1926.
10. Raymond J. Lawrence, Jr., *The Poisoning of Eros: Sexual Values in Conflict,* Augustine Moore Press, 1989, p. 25.

a particular man, adultery was essentially a prohibition of the invasion of a man's sphere. Adultery did not apply to married men and their liaisons with unattached women, such as widows, concubines or maidservants.

The Old Testament, as a whole, contains an abundance of sexual allusions and sexually explicit stories. But its concern about sexual issues is a concern about covenant and interpersonal responsibility within it.

The biblical commandment against adultery has little to do with sex as such, has nothing to do with monogamy, and certainly has nothing to do with sexual purity as an ideal. The invasion or intrusion into a private domain in contravention of an existing covenant is the concern that motivates the Torah's prohibition of adultery. As Paul Lehmann (following Luther) points out, the commandment means, "Thou shalt not break in and break up a marriage."[11]

Neither the Jews nor Luther were concerned as we tend to be today about the specific question of sex outside of the bounds of marriage. The commandment proscribing adultery in fact applied only to married women, not to men in their relationships with unattached women. Both the Jews and Luther were concerned that the community respect and protect marital covenants.[12]

Marriage author David R. Mace writes,

When we consider premarital and extramarital sex relations, we encounter a situation that can be quite puzzling, until we examine it in the light of the Hebrew values ...

The word adultery is often used in the Old Testament. For the Hebrews, however, it had a very different meaning from what it has in our world of today ... A Hebrew man, married or unmarried, could have sexual intercourse with any available woman without censure or penalty.

That sounds very permissive. However, the puzzle was to find an available woman! ... Almost every woman in Hebrew society was ... under the authority of ... some particular man. In her early years, the authority was that of her father, who was responsible for her virginity until he could get her married, usually soon after puberty. A married woman was under her husband's au-

11. Paul Lehmann, *The Decalogue and the Parameters of a Human Future,* Association of Clinical Pastoral Education Conference, 1981, p. 41.
12. Lawrence, *Op. Cit,* pp. 256-257.

thority. A widow was under the care of a son …

Adultery, therefore, was for the Hebrews a sexual offense in which a man violated, in effect, the property rights of some other man, and the law had to settle it between them.[13]

---

13. David R. Mace, *The Sacred Fire,* Abingdon Press, 1986, pp. 32-33.

Chapter 11

Lust in Matthew 5:28

But I say to you, that whosoever looks on a woman to lust after her has committed adultery with her already in his heart (Matthew 5:28).

Few there would be who are not familiar with this verse! Most in Christendom would have us believe that this passage actually reads as follows:

Whosoever looks on a woman has committed adultery with her already in his heart (Matthew 5:28).

They make the act of *"looking"* to be the key issue of the verse. They confuse the difference between *"look"* and *"lust after."*[1] The issue was "looking" with purpose and intent – *i.e.*, "looking" on a woman **"to** *lust after her."*

The average Christian's failure to distinguish the difference between "looking" and "lusting" is identical to the way that they fail to distinguish the difference between "drinking" and "drunkenness."

What does it mean to look at a woman *"to lust after her?"* Is this lusting *"after her"* a simple thought, or does it indicate a thought of pursuit?

I recommend caution here, for if we claim it only requires a look, or thought, to commit adultery – then all men would be immediately guilty. Why so? Because this is the way of our nature: this is the way that God has designed us to be. God has made man with the innate appreciation for, and attraction to female beauty!

---

1. By missing the emphasis upon "lust after," does the modern day moralist suggest that a blind man cannot lust after a woman in his heart?

We shall see clearly that this lusting *"after her"* of which our Lord spoke, is the desiring for an opportunity to have an illicit sexual encounter with *another's wife*. The Lord was not talking about the act of actually having her, but his merely attempting or waiting for the opportunity. This is what would have qualified him as guilty of having *"committed adultery with her already in his heart."*

The issue is *"in his heart,"* for had the opportunity arrived, he would have indulged his desires. So it is that *intent* with another man's wife is all that is necessary here. Committing the actual act is not necessary if the *intent* is there. This is what Jesus was referring to when he spoke of lusting *"after"* a woman.

Make no mistake: it is indeed a *married* woman that is the object of man's attention here, for it is only with a *married* woman that *adultery* can be committed. Jesus was talking about the illicit desire of a man's heart toward *another man's wife*.

Adultery does not come from the *eyes*, it is from the *heart*:

> *For out of the heart proceeds … adulteries* (Matthew 15:19; c.f. Mark 7:21).

It is possible for a man to look at any woman (even a married woman) and appreciate her wonderful design and beauty, and in doing so give thanks to God for His gift of sexuality. While another man looks at a beautiful *married* woman and can only see that which he desires to have for himself – what he can steal from her husband.[2]

This is the sin spoken of by Peter, *"having eyes full of adultery"* (II Peter 2:14).

Having a desire for the opposite sex – or being attracted to them and finding them appealing and compelling, appreciating their beautiful forms – are not wrong or improper desires in themselves. These were all placed within man by **God Himself.** The problem arises when a man desires to *possess* that which does not belong to him.

> *Unto the pure all things are pure: but unto them who are defiled and unbelieving is nothing pure; but even their mind and conscience is defiled* (Titus 1:15).

---

2. "David looks across the way at a beautiful woman bathing. If the story had stopped there, in verse 2 [II Samuel 11], when David was only looking, there would be no harm, no foul." (T.J. Hornsby, *Sex Texts from the Bible*, p. 52).

If a man looks upon a woman desiring an opportunity to be with her sexually, and she belongs to another man, and he would indeed accept such an occasion with her if one were available, that constitutes adultery. He has already made the deceitful decision in his heart. All that remains is for the opportunity to be presented. That is the sin of adultery in the heart, and it is wrong.

Religionists would actually make our text read:

> Whosoever looks on a woman has committed fornication with her already in his heart (Matthew 5:28 – Religionist Version).

They change the *act* in the verse to merely "looking," and the *sin* to "fornication." They do this because *they* have defined "fornication" as a large catch-all for any and all sexual "immorality." This passage has *nothing* to do with fornication. It has to do with the sin of *adultery* – adultery taking place in the heart.

There is also nothing in the passage about how much or little clothing the woman is wearing. Is nudity necessary for a man to *"lust after"* a woman with adultery in his heart? Could one *"lust after"* a woman who was fully dressed? Is it possible? Certainly!

Is the reverse possible? Could one view a woman totally nude and *not* "lust after" her with adultery in his heart? Not desiring to steal her from her husband? Is it possible? Certainly! Again, *"lust"* for adultery is a heart attitude, regardless of the clothing, or lack of clothing worn by a woman.

If you look at a woman so as to desire a chance to be with her sexually, and she does *not* have a husband, then you have *not* committed a sin. It could *not* be adultery, for she has *no* husband against whom adultery would be committed! What do you have then? You have a qualification for marriage. This is because lust is good biblical grounds for a marriage (see I Corinthians 7)!

LOOKING AT A BEAUTIFUL WOMAN

Regarding this subject one author aptly writes,

> Human nature is such that *every* normal male is sexually attracted to a pretty woman. He doesn't have to "work up" an attraction, it is simply *there*. It is *automatic* for a man to delight in the sight of a beautiful woman and to have a strong sense of her sexuality. It is all *part of one package* …

If a man looks at a beautiful woman, is sexually aroused and is moved to ask the woman for a date, has he sinned? Is a man's delight in a woman's sexuality legitimate as part of his desire to marry her? …

A man is aroused by the physical/sexual beauty of a married woman. Is this *arousal* sin? That is, if a man is sexually excited by the beauty of a *married* woman, yet has no desire and forms no intention to take her away from her husband, has he sinned? Where is the sin – in the look? In the sexual excitement? What biblical word or phrase describes this act as sin? Is being *sexually aroused* the same as *desiring to possess* a person? Isn't there a difference between looking with delight at a thing versus "lusting" after it? …

It may now be apparent to wives, that when their husband "checks out" a beautiful woman he is not somehow being "mentally unfaithful" to her, or wishing he had married someone else, or no longer thinks she is beautiful, or no longer loves her … If a husband looks appreciatively at another woman the wife need not feel hurt as though she has somehow become less in his eyes.[3]

EVERY MAN'S BATTLE?

Does every man (or every woman) have an evil struggle with their own sexuality? If so, they need not experience this struggle!

Did God give men and women a sex drive as a plague? Absolutely not! What an awful trick to play, if this was so. Sexuality is God's wonderful gift to be *enjoyed*, not battled.

Is an internal battle what God intended as the normal Christian life? Are we fighting an internal civil war? Are we wrestling against ourselves? The answer to these questions is "NO!"

What a joy to be free from sin *and* its bondage, and what a joy to be free from religion and its bondage as well – free to walk in righteousness, honesty and love, and in the liberty that is in Christ; free to live fully persuaded before Him.

---

3. Philo Thelos, *Divine Sex: Liberating Sex from Religious Tradition*, 2002, pp. 128, vi, 113-114.

FOR FREEDOM

We will close this chapter with these valuable words:

> The Apostle Paul teaches us that the blood of Jesus Christ sets us free *"for freedom"* (Galatians 5:1). *"For freedom"* means Jesus did not die for *theoretical* liberty. He intends that we *experience* it. Freedom that is merely talked about, written about, spoken about, *but never experienced* is not freedom at all. Honoring Christ requires that we *use* the liberty purchased for us at so high a price …
>
> We *dishonor* Christ if we live in fear and dread and *refuse* to experience what we might otherwise enjoy, on the basis of submitting, even *reluctantly*, to some human code, tradition or law, or by remaining bound to an illegitimate system under which we were raised from our youth. In such a situation we honor purely human laws and traditions *more highly* than we honor Christ's blood-bought freedom.
>
> To live under a cloud of "what I have always believed" or resist going into freedom on the basis of other people's opinions is dishonoring to the One whose horrific death purchased our freedom. Our freedom cost far too much for us not to use it in whatever areas we desire to do so.
>
> Once gaining liberty at the cost of Jesus' blood we must *"stand firm and do not be subject again to a yoke of slavery"* (Galatians 5:1). This admonition requires us to *refuse* to give up freedom won for us by Christ's blood. No human has God's permission to return to or continue to live under any bondage from which the blood of Christ sets us free. Again we say, the *price is too high*. Embracing Jesus Christ and His work on the cross requires us to embrace the freedom His death purchased for us there … We must avoid being *"entangled again in a yoke of bondage."* Once escaping bondage we are *obligated* to leave and not go back.[4]

---

4. *Ibid.,* p. 225-227.

Chapter 12

Fornication in the Bible

Flee fornication (I Corinthians 6:18, *King James Version*).

Flee from prostitution (I Corinthians 6:18, *Concordant Literal Translation*).

Most of Christendom is completely ignorant of the biblical meaning of the word "fornication." When Paul says, *"Flee fornication,"* to what exactly was he referring? From what was he specifically pleading with the Corinthian believers to flee?

JUST WHAT IS FORNICATION?

As one approaches the Scriptures for a biblical definition, they might well be surprised to find out what fornication actually is.

Many Bible words have lost their true meaning through years of relentless religious tradition. Fornication is clearly such a word. It has been well molded to suit Christendom's moralistic agenda.

The real key in regaining a biblical definition of words is to allow the Scriptures themselves to define the meaning of its own words.

WORD MEANINGS

Loyal Hurley wrote in *The Outcome of Infinite Grace,*

In all languages, it is usage that determines meaning ... Since usage always determines meaning, biblical usage, certainly, always determines biblical meaning.

William Barclay echoed this resounding testimony,

> If we fail to study the meaning of the words of Scripture, then we will be in very serious danger of making Scripture mean what we want it to mean, and not what God wants it to mean.[1]

Often, in this process, one of the more helpful principles that we can follow in learning the accurate meaning of a biblical word is what is known as the *first mention principle.*

THE FIRST MENTION

The *principle of first mention* declares that the first time God uses a word in Scripture, He often gives us vital and foundational keys to its definition – a meaning that will carry throughout the rest of the Bible.

The very first mention of *"fornication"* is found in II Chronicles:

> *Moreover he made high places in the mountains of Judah, and caused the inhabitants of Jerusalem to commit fornication, and compelled Judah thereto* (II Chronicles 21:11).

The *"high places"* spoken of here, and throughout the Old Testament, were places of idolatrous, pagan worship. Simply put, we can see from this first mention of fornication that it is a sin committed in the act of idol worship. Particularly, it is the sin of sexually using one's body in the worship of a false deity.

Our text, *"Flee fornication,"* was written to the Corinthians. Interestingly enough, in the city of Corinth, the pagan, cultic temple prostitutes would seduce the men to come into the temple to sexually worship the god of fertility.

Our sexuality was graciously given to us by God. Just as with any other aspect of who we are, we are to use our sexuality in honor and worship of Him. The Corinthian believers were being tempted to take their God-given sexuality and use it in the worship of false gods.

---

1. William Barclay, *Daily Celebration*, p. 21.

THE CORINTHIAN CONTEXT

One author sheds some much-needed light on the situation that existed in the city of Corinth.

> In ancient Corinth, having sex with a [temple] prostitute was an act of idolatry. Sex was an act of worship that bonded a man to a pagan goddess.

> In pagan cultures, fornication and idolatry went hand in hand. Having sex with a cult prostitute was a way of worshiping one's favorite god or goddess …

> Corinth was famous for prostitution. The Temple of Venus was the most magnificent building in the city. The temple employed a thousand prostitutes financed with public funds. Many early converts to Christianity continued their old practices, which included going to the temple and engaging in orgies dedicated to the worship of Venus. They saw nothing wrong with this. Paul, however, warned them to "flee fornication."

> Many have taken Paul's warning out of context. The words "flee fornication" have been widely misappropriated, battering potential transgressors like a ministerial billy-club.

> Meanwhile, Christendom seems oblivious to what fornication meant in biblical times …

> A Corinthian prostitute regarded her body as a temple of Venus. … This should not be taken as a *carte blanche* condemnation of prostitution because it is possible for a prostitute to practice her profession ethically and still enter the Kingdom[2]

Other authors have also written concerning this important historical perspective.

> In the times of Corinthian opulence and prosperity, it is said that the shrine of Venus was attended by no less than one thousand female slaves dedicated to her service as courtesans. These priestesses of Venus contributed not a little to the wealth and luxury of the city. – *Anthon's Classical Dictionary.* Article: Corinthus[3]

---

2. Tom Gruber, *What the Bible Really Says About Sex*, 2001, Trafford Publishing, pp. 22, 44-47.
3. Cited by James Campbell, *A History and Philosophy of Marriage,* Patriarch Publishing House, 2007, p. 50.

Strabo, in his great work on Geography, in speaking of the temple of Venus in Corinth says, "There were more than a thousand harlots, the slaves of the temple, who, in honor of the goddess, prostituted themselves to all comers for hire, and through these the city was crowded, and became wealthy." – Bulwer's *History of Athens,* Book 8, p. 151.[4]

THE WORD ITSELF

Now let's take a look at the word *"fornication"* itself.

The Greek word used to translate *"fornication"* is *porneia* (and its various forms). *"Porneia"* means to sell, and refers to slaves bought and sold for pagan, cultic prostitution.

In fact, the root of our English word *"fornication"* is *"fornix,"* which all etymological resources agree means *"a brothel."* In the biblical sense this was not just any brothel: it was a pagan, cultic brothel used in cultic sexual worship.

Raymond J. Lawrence confirms this, stating that,

> In Greek, *porneia* has the root meaning of prostitution ... When Paul writes in I Corinthians 10:8 that 23,000 were slain in one day for *porneia,* he is making reference to **cultic sexual practice** ... (An allusion to Numbers 25:1, 9 and Exodus 32:6.)

Idolatry, or competing religious cult, is the concern here, not sexuality as such. Similarly, in I Corinthians 6:9-10, 15-18, Paul links *porneia* with idolatry. He compares linking oneself with a religious prostitute.

> *Know you not that the unrighteous shall not inherit the kingdom of God? Be not deceived: neither fornicators [pornoi], nor idolaters, nor adulterers, nor effeminate, nor abusers of themselves with mankind, Nor thieves, nor covetous, nor drunkards, nor revilers, nor extortioners, shall inherit the kingdom of God ... Know you not that your bodies are the members of Christ? shall I then take the members of Christ, and make them the members of an harlot [pornoi]? God forbid. What? know you not that he who is joined to a harlot [pornes] is one body? "For two," said He, "shall be one flesh." But he who is joined unto the Lord is one spirit.*

---

4. *Ibid.*

Flee fornication [porneia]. Every sin that a man does is without the body; but he who commits fornication [porneia] sins against his own body.

This suggests that Paul was thinking … of *porneia* as a form of prostitution … associated with pagan cultic practices, as for example the cult of Venus. By no stretch of the imagination could this be taken as any kind of comment about the question of sex outside of marriage.[5]

The famed *Halley's Bible Handbook* tells us concerning I Corinthians 6:9-20,

Venus was the principal deity of Corinth. Her temple was one of the most magnificent buildings in the city. In it a thousand priestesses, public prostitutes, were kept, at public expense, there always ready for immoral indulgence, as worship to their goddess.[6]

What a draw that must have been for these pagan temples! Cultic sex on the premises for everyone! No wonder Paul would have had to address this issue with the Corinthian believers! This is because they were drawn to the temple for cultic sexual indulgences with the priestesses of Venus. This is what Paul was dealing with.

It does violation to the biblical text to assume I Corinthians 6:9 is anything other than cultic sexual worship. We alter its clear scriptural meaning if we make it "premarital," or any other "immoral" sex activity (erroneously, of itself, called *"fornication").*

This is especially true since this is *not* the context of the discussion, either of this chapter or of the surrounding chapters. The context of I Corinthians 6 is the problem with the Temple of Aphrodite. Sex with those pagan, cultic prostitutes was idolatrous. Interestingly enough, six of the eleven times the word *"fornication"* is used in Paul's epistles are found in Paul's writings to the Corinthians!

CLEAR BIBLICAL DEFINITION

As believers we must allow God to define His Own words. God does clearly define fornication in I Corinthians 10:7-8, 14 when it is compared to its companion context of Numbers 25:1-9. The student of Scripture should take the necessary time to compare these two passages and their important relationship to each

---

5. Raymond J. Lawrence, Jr., *The Poisoning of Eros: Sexual Values in Conflict,* Augustine Moore Press, 1989, pp. 35-36.

6. Henry H. Halley, *Halley's Bible Handbook,* Zondervan, p. 595.

other. One will soon learn that this use of sex in the worship of false gods is plainly what *"fornication"* is all about.

> *Neither be idolaters, as were some of them; as it is written, "The people sat down to eat and drink, and rose up to play." Neither let us commit fornication, as some of them committed, and fell in one day three and twenty thousand ... Wherefore, my dearly beloved, flee from idolatry* (I Corinthians 10:7-8, 14).

Paul here clearly is referring to Numbers 25. Don't settle for the religious system's imposed definition. Read carefully to see for yourself the biblical context and definition of *"fornication."*

> *And Israel abode in Shittim, and the people began to commit whoredom with the daughters of Moab. And they called the people unto the sacrifices of their gods: and the people did eat, and bowed down to their gods. And Israel joined himself unto Baalpeor: and the anger of the LORD was kindled against Israel. And the LORD said unto Moses, "Take all the heads of the people, and hang them up before the LORD against the sun, that the fierce anger of the LORD may be turned away from Israel." And Moses said unto the judges of Israel, "Slay every one his men who were joined unto Baalpeor." And, behold, one of the children of Israel came and brought unto his brothers a Midianitish woman in the sight of Moses, and in the sight of all the congrega-tion of the children of Israel, who were weeping before the door of the taber-nacle of the congregation. And when Phinehas, the son of Eleazar, the son of Aaron the priest, saw it, he rose up from among the congregation, and took a javelin in his hand; And he went after the man of Israel into the tent, and thrust both of them through, the man of Israel, and the woman through her belly. So the plague was stayed from the children of Israel. And those who died in the plague were twenty-four thousand* (Numbers 25:1-9).

This passage brings amazing clarity upon the subject. It brings a precision that sheds great light on other passages that utilize the word *fornication*. Now, note elsewhere for example, the use of the word *fornication* in the apostolic decree found in Acts 15:20.

> *But that we write unto them, that they abstain from pollutions of idols, and from fornication, and from things strangled, and from blood.*[7]

---

7. "So also Acts 15:19 and 21:25 would seem to support a connotation of *porneia* as cultic activity. It is included in a list of ritual or cultic prohibitations ..." (Lawrence, *Op. Cit.,* p. 36).

The bottom line of this injunction is *idolatry*.

E.W. Bullinger writes concerning this passage,

> In many cases the rites of heathenism involved uncleanness as an act of worship. Cp. Numbers 25:1-15. Probably the worship of the golden calf was of that character (Exodus 32:6, 25).[8]

Another author writes,

> Fornication deals with spiritual mixture and is not the same as adultery. Jezebel, a woman in the church of Thyatira described in the book of Revelation, symbolized fornication because she led the people into deception (Revelation 2:20) ... Fornication is a spiritual sin, while adultery is a flesh sin.[9]

This pagan, cultic prostitution is what God prohibited in the book of Deuteronomy:

> There shall be no whore of the daughters of Israel, nor a sodomite of the sons of Israel (Deuteronomy 23:17).

One of the Hebrew words for *"whore"* and *"harlot"* is *Strong's Hebrew Lexicon* #6948, *qadeshah,* meaning "a female devotee (*i.e.,* prostitute)" and is the feminine form of *"qadesh"* (#6945). *Qadesh* is defined by Strong as "a sacred person, *i.e.,* (technically) a (male) devotee (by prostitution) to licentious idolatry."

> These words mean quite simply a holy woman or a holy man and referred ... to the cult of male and female temple prostitutes. The *Revised Standard Version* of the Bible renders this word as "cult prostitute."[10]

8. E.W. Bullinger, *The Companion Bible.*
9. Earl Paulk, *Sex Is God's Idea,* K Dimension Publishers, 1985, p. 141.
10. John Shelby Spong, *Living in Sin,* Harper, San Franscisco, 1988, p. 143.

Chapter 13

Sexual Stimuli

I will praise You; for I am fearfully and wonderfully made: marvelous are Your works; and that my soul knows right well (Psalms 139:14).

Know you that the LORD He is God: it is He Who has made us, and not we ourselves ... (Psalms 100:3).

Many believers struggle when it comes to issues of sexual stimuli. Such arousal comes in a variety of avenues and in a wide range of degrees.

The man is especially designed by God to be attracted and drawn to the female and her form. He is keyed sexually to the sight of her. Even the scene of a woman complementarily outfitting her feminine figure can be quite arousing (let alone when she accents or amplifies it). Then of course there is erotic art, writing, photography, and film.

What about sexual stimuli as it relates to the believer? Is it wrong for the believer to have such stimuli? Is it wrong to be sexually stimulated? At its very root, is it unnatural and ungodly? or is it a natural, godly design?

We will not specifically be addressing the effects of sexual stimuli upon the female, but upon the male. We will focus upon the man because this is where God places His emphasis. This is not to say that such stimuli have no bearing on the woman – for they do; but God has designed and made her for the man.

To help us in our consideration of the whole area of sexual stimuli, we will now look at two words often associated with it: "erotica" and "pornography."

"EROTICA"

A definition

The word *erotic* is defined as:

> Of or concerning sexual love and desire; amatory. Tending to arouse sexual desire –*American Heritage Dictionary*

> Related to sexual desire and pleasure – *Cambridge Dictionary*

Although the word "erotic" does not appear in Noah Webster's 1828 dictionary, the word "erotical" does. He defines it as

> Pertaining to love; treating of love – *An American Dictionary of the English Language*

An Etymological Definition

At the root of our word "erotic" is the Greek word *eros* which is the word for sexual love.[1]

Consider the words used to define "erotic." It concerns "sexual love and desire."

Is sexual love and desire godly or ungodly? Isn't God the author of sexuality and its accompanying desire?

Sex is God's idea. It is all His design. Man did not "think it up." Sex honors God greatly.

Much of what we think we know about our sexuality (including stimuli) is based upon cultural and religious tradition. Most saints live their lives in bondage to such tradition.

Erotica, so commonly suppressed and dismissed, are actually based upon godly design, rather than so-called "sinful passion." The so-called "Everyman's Battle" is, in fact, not designed to be a battle, but a precious gift. Believers have been

---

1. Robert K. Barnhart, *Barnhart Concise Dictionary of Etymology*, Eric Partridge, *Origins: A Short Etymological Dictionary of Modern English*,.

wrongfully deceived concerning one of God's greatest gifts to man. As a result, lives have been scarred and damaged.

"PORNOGRAPHY"

A definition

The word *pornography* is defined as:

> Sexually explicit pictures, writing, or other material ... – *American Heritage Dictionary*

Based on this root definition of "pornography," the Bible would clearly be viewed as a pornographic book. It literally is filled with "erotic" and "pornographic" material. For this reason, in the Victorian era many parts of the Bible were actually banned from being read.

Even Noah Webster wrote concerning what he viewed as the *indecency* of the *King James Version:*

> In no respect does the present version of the Scriptures require amendments, more than in the use of many words and phrases which cannot now be uttered, especially in promiscuous company, without violence to decency. In early stages of society, when men are savage or half civilized, such terms are not offensive: but in the present state of refinement, the utterance of many words and passages of our version is not to be endured; and it is well known that some parents do not permit their children to read the Scriptures, without prescribing to them the chapters.[2]

An Etymological Definition

When we come to the actual root of our word "pornography" we gain a different usage of the word. The root is the Greek word *pornea.*

> Etymologically, the literal meaning of *pornea* is *prostitution*. The Greek word for prostitute is *porne,* which is where the word *pornography* comes from. The word pornography simply means *a story of a prostitute*. According to this definition, the Disney film *Pretty Woman* is pornographic.[3]

---

2. Noah Webster, *Introduction to Webster's Bible,* 1833
3. Tom Gruber, *What the Bible Really Says About Sex,* 2001, Trafford Publishing, pp. 22, 44-47.

To this we might add that by the technical etymological definition of the root word, the Bible's story of Rahab the harlot is "pornographic" also – being the story of a prostitute.

A BROAD PRACTICAL DEFINITION

One author makes an attempt to give us a broad practical working definition:

> … Pornography in print or film is *no worse* than *walking* pornography – living, walking, talking, pornography that appears in the semi-nude – in the form of scanty apparel on the streets, in the schools, the office, the factory, at the swimming pools, etc.[4]

In the Bible we find the literary artwork of sexual "erotica." The Song of Solomon is a prime example of the expression of such sexual passion. It contains the passion of a husband and his wife, describing each other in their love making. It is a very detailed and graphic presentation. Song of Solomon demonstrates that such eroticism, in and of itself, is not sinful.

Why would God inspire such an erotic love story between a man and his wife? There is a question for the religionists, and the Victorian-styled moralists! Of course their answer would be to allegorize the book, but even the allegory, it must be admitted, would have been based upon the sexual love.

We recognize that the more sexual content a writing contains, the more it would tend to arouse the reader. This is because sexual arousal – sometimes called passion – is an emotion.

Have you ever watched a scary movie and experienced the emotion of fear? Likewise a story with sexual content causes the reader to experience the emotion of sexual arousal, desire, or passion.

As with any other passion, it is not a sin to experience the passion of sexual arousal. Sin related to passion is only found in what is done as a result of that excitement. In fact, passion can be used to the glory of God. If the believer used "erotica" found in the Bible (or elsewhere!) and applied their aroused passions to their spouse, this would obviously not be sin.

---

4. Robert McCurry, *Walking Pornography*, The Temple Times, (republished in *The Forgotten Truths*, Issue #53, Grace Bible Church, Hampton, VA, 1985, Clyde L. Pilkington, Jr., editor).

"Pornography" is a word that gets thrown around a lot. It is one of those "dirty" words that often are used to impose religious and moral intimidation and bondage. Obtaining a real working definition of "pornography" is not as simple as it may appear on the surface. Even in the arena of law, there has been much difficulty in defining terms such as "obscenity" and "pornography," largely leaving it up to "community standards." As one author upon the subject frankly admits,

> The definition of both pornography and eroticism is difficult to free from subjectivism.[5]

ARE "EROTICA" AND "PORNOGRAPHY" WRONG?

Since it obviously is hard to define what "erotica" and "pornography" actually are, as a result it also may be difficult to view them as "good" or "evil," making it a little hard to answer that question without some qualification. Moreover, since these words, as we use them, are not "biblical" words as such, it makes it even the more difficult. A similar word might be "sex." It does not appear in the Bible either.

One might just as well ask, "Is 'sex' wrong?" For many it, too, may be a little hard to answer without some qualification.

The principle of law is *"touch not; taste not; handle not"* (Colossians 2:21). By contrast, Paul's principles of grace are unmistakably clear:

Unto the pure all things are pure ... (Titus 1:15).

... There is nothing unclean of itself ... (Romans 14:14).

All things are lawful unto me ... (I Corinthians 6:12; I Corinthians 10:23).

This last principle Paul gives twice when writing to the Corinthians: *"All things are lawful unto me ..."* This truth is tempered with three "buts" – the spirit of expediency, edification and emancipation:

EXPEDIENCY

... but all things are not expedient (I Corinthians 10:23).

5. Frank Bottomley, *Attitudes To The Body In Western Christendom*, Lepus Books, 1979, p. 147.

EDIFICATION

... but all things edify not (I Corinthians 10:23).

EMANCIPATION

... but I will not be brought under the power of any (I Corinthians 6:12).

PORNOGRAPHY IS A QUESTION OF GEOGRAPHY

In the play *The Teahouse of the August Moon* we have the following adapted foreign observation portrayed:

In Okinawa, to wash yourself in a public bath with a nude lady is quite proper.

In America, a statue of a nude lady in a park would win a prize. But a nude lady in the flesh in park would win a penalty.

Conclusion? Pornography must be a question of geography.[6]

THE BELIEVER IS FREE

Stand fast therefore in the liberty wherewith Christ has made us free, and be not entangled again with the yoke of bondage (Galatians 5:1).

Christ has made the believer free – free from the bondage of legalism. The believer is free to enjoy life. *All* things are lawful unto him, under God's guiding spirit of grace: expediency, edification and emancipation.

Anything that hurts another person is wrong.

... For all the law is fulfilled in one word, even in this; "You shall love your neighbor as yourself" (Galatians 5:14).

Anything that could not be done in honor and worship of God is wrong.

Whether therefore you eat, or drink, or whatsoever you do, do all to the

---

6. *The Teahouse of the August Moon* by John Patrick, adapted from the novel by Vern Sneider (Dramatists Play Services, 1957), p. 6.

glory of God (I Corinthians 10:31).

And whatsoever you do in word or deed, do all in the name of the Lord Jesus, giving thanks to God and the Father by Him (Colossians 3:17).

And whatsoever you do, do it heartily, as to the Lord, and not unto men (Colossians 3:23).

Anything that cannot be done in faith is wrong.

And he who doubts is damned if he eats, because he eats not of faith: for whatsoever is not of faith is sin (Romans 14:23).

This spirit of grace applies to all the details of life, including our sexuality, even extending to the area of sexual stimuli.

POTENTIAL POSITIVE EFFECT

Since many passages of Scripture have been viewed by believers to be "obscene" or "pornographic" throughout history, we would need to consider the possibility of a potential positive effect that "erotica" may have.

One Christian author dares to pose a counter viewpoint to religious thought:[7]

> Certainly, viewing "pornography" or anything else can be expected to influence the thinking of the viewer. But is it necessarily a bad influence? Letha Scanzoni thinks not:
>
>> What should we say to the Christian woman who, after attending with her husband an X-rated movie for the first time, said she wished they had seen it fifteen years ago? She said it would have helped them so much in their sexual relationship. She had been a problem throughout their marriage because she had felt so inhibited and afraid of certain techniques.[8]

For this particular wife, what would be viewed by the religionist and moralist as only "evil" and "wicked" was used as an education for her marital life – a life that had been held in the bondage of Gnostic intimidation and fear was helped in her wifely duty of *"due benevolence."* By what Biblical "law" shall we discount her

7. Robertson McQuilkin, *An Introduction To Biblical Ethics*, Tyndale House Publishers, 1989.
8. Letha Scanzoni, *See No Evil, The Other Side*, 1978, p. 23.

experience? What divine rules[9] shall we impose upon her and her husband? How dare we or others seek to play the role of God in their lives.

STATISTICS OF CHRISTIAN USE

We must realize that various forms of "erotica" have *always* been a part of human life and behavior – *even* among Christians. Our modern day examples are no exception!

Some recent research brings the relevance of our study of this topic to light.

A few years ago, *Promise Keepers* conducted a survey at one of their events. 50% of the 50,000 men responding admitted to viewing pornography the week before they came to the *Promise Keeper* event.[10]

Barna research found that 60 percent of Christian men actively seek out pornography.[11]

Half of all adults stated that watching a movie with explicit sexual behavior is morally acceptable. That view was shared by three out of ten born-again adults.[12]

In a *Christianity Today* poll, one third of Christian pastors surveyed said they have visited sexually explicit web sites.[13]

I think we all know that statistics can be poorly taken, confusing and manipulated. Still, think about what we have read. These statistics at least merit our attention.

Let's take the first statistic. 50,000 men gather at a *Promise Keepers* meeting. These are men who have some passion, or at least interest, in dedication to family values. These are men who had gathered out from among many various religious denominations. Their interest, time and expense to attend the meeting would regard them as the "cream of the crop." Yet half of them were willing to admit

---

9. Rules - "We think that the Bible is our source of rules for sex. The truth is, we pick and choose rules from the Bible depending on which ones agree with already-held societal beliefs about sexual right and wrong." – T.J. Hornsby, *Sex Texts from the Bible*, p. 162.
10. GTO Family Ministries; *The Hidden Enemy of Marriage,* Focus on the Family Broadcast; Laurie Hall *An Affair of the Mind.*
11. FaithLinks: The Living Church Foundation.
12. Barna Research Group , 2001.
13. FaithLinks: The Living Church Foundation.

that they had viewed "pornography the week before they came to the *Promise Keeper* event."

Let's also consider the last statistic. One third of Christian pastors surveyed were willing to admit that they had visited sexually explicit websites.

What do these statistics reveal to us? A couple of things; first it tells us that the *position* of the moral religionist is at odds with their *practice*. It also tells us that in spite of their supposed *position* against erotic stimuli – with its intimidation of fear and shame – there was something driving the interest of pastors and leading laymen. What was this something? The natural male design.[14, 15]

Before closing this look into sexual stimuli, we will share a few portions from the pen of others.

FEMALE BEAUTY

One author discusses the differences between sin and appreciation, and personal choices and freedom.

> Toleration for the appreciation of feminine beauty without sinful desire differs, just as tolerance for the appreciation of a desirable object without coveting it differs. If the sexual stimulation of the typical worldly magazine is too much for a person to control, he should not read it even though it might be harmless to another.[16]

AN ANALOGY

A Christian author offers us an interesting analogy.

> Consider the parallel between the bottled water and the "porn" industry. We blithely pay a dollar or more for a gallon of bottled water. Mind-boggling, isn't it. Shouldn't everyone have plenty of pure water – ***free?***

14. Many are surprised to find out that there is a phrase "Christian pornography" found in literature dealing with the history of this subject. Does such a phrase as "Christian pornography" seem strange or appalling to you? Does it even seem contradictory? Is it possible that Christendom is much more under the influence of moralistic religion than we have ever realized?

15. "The controversial Presidential Commission on Pornography appointed in 1967 concluded that no personal change or adverse effects in youth or adults from viewing pornography could be demonstrated and therefore recommended that all legal restrictions on all pornography be lifted." McQuilkin, *Op. Cit.*

16. *Ibid.*

Who is the culprit – the customer? No, he's got a legitimate need.

What about the store – is the store the bad guy? No, the store supplies a needed product.

Is the bottled water company to blame? Of course not. Who can blame a company for selling a legitimate product for a profit?

So who *is* to blame? Obviously, it's the scoundrel polluting our water! He's the one creating the market. If there were plenty of free, pure water, bottled water companies wouldn't have anybody to sell to.

The same is true of the "porn" industry. The devil in disguise is that hallowed, finger-wagging crusader who pollutes our minds with the propaganda that sex is evil. … For centuries, misguided Christians have been imposing their false legalistic rules of sexual suppression on a weary public. That's why *Hustler* and *Playboy* have such a hot market. What should be freely available is condemned as a menace to society.[17]

HEAVEN-BORN IMPULSES

Another Christian author wrote in 1869,

Shall these heaven-born impulses of nature be regarded, or must they be re-pressed? … Implanted for the noblest purposes within our breasts, interwoven with the very fibers of our being, the laws of God and of nature unquestion-ably demand their indulgence.

In plainer terms, the laws of God and of nature clearly indicate that every man and every woman, possessing sufficient health and vitality to experience the passion of love, is benefited by its proper gratification; and those laws both allow and invite every one to enjoy it in its full fruition.

A man is not wholly a man, nor a woman wholly a woman, who has never experienced the ecstasies of gratified love. Those men and women, who are spending their most vigorous period of life in cold and barren celibacy, without ever having yielded to the warm desires of reproduction, are living, every moment, in debt to their Creator and to the commonwealth of mankind. They

---

17. Tom Gruber, *What the Bible Really Says About Sex,* Trafford Publishing, 2001, pp. 52-53.

have never fulfilled some of the most important purposes of their being.[18]

We will conclude this chapter with two more quotations.

AGAPE AND EROS

Christianity's tendency to steer clear of the erotic has often set the spiritual over against human culture and experience. ... The relationship between the different forms of love [agape and eros] should not be seen as opposition or choice. In the end, eros just as much as agape is expressive of the same drive toward union with the One ... God is erotic power properly understood and is the erotic power between people. God is our capacity to love revealing itself in the matrix of all human relations.[19]

EROS AND GOD

If the eros quality of love with respect to God is rejected, the consequence of this rejection is that love toward God becomes an impossible concept ... replaced by mere obedience to God.[20]

18. James Campbell, *A History and Philosophy of Marriage,* Patriarch Publishing House, 2007, p. 25.

19. Philip Sheldrake, *Befriending Our Desires: Unity of Agape and Eros,* 1994, pp. 39-40.

20. Paul Tillich, *Love, Power and Justice,* 1954, p. 29.

Chapter 14

Euphemisms

There is a lot of sexual content in the Bible, but more often than not it is veiled by the usage of a figure of speech called *euphemism*.

The *Oxford English Dictionary* defines *euphemism* as,

> A mild or less direct word substituted for one that is harsh or blunt when referring to something unpleasant or embarrassing.

The *American Heritage Dictionary* defines it as,

> The act or an example of substituting a mild, indirect, or vague term for one considered harsh, blunt, or offensive.

Through the usage of *euphemisms* much of the sexuality of the Bible is actually hidden to many.

All of us are aware of some of the *euphemisms* of the Bible, though we may not know them by that name. For example, one of the most common sexual *euphemisms* in the Bible is the word *"know."* To *"know"* someone in a biblical sense can mean to have sexual intercourse with them.

Note the following examples:

> Adam **knew** Eve his wife; and she conceived, and bore Cain, and said, "I have gotten a man from the LORD" (Genesis 4:1).

> Adam **knew** his wife again; and she bore a son, and called his name Seth (Genesis 4:25).

Cain **knew** his wife; and she conceived, and bore Enoch (Genesis 4:17).

Then said Mary unto the angel, "How shall this be, seeing I **know** not a man?" (Luke 1:34).

In each of these cases the word *"knew"* or *"know"* is a reference to what is sometimes referred to as "carnal knowledge," or sexual intercourse. The word *"know"* is just one of many *euphemisms* that are of a sexual nature.

Our purpose here is to awaken the student of Scripture to the reality of *euphemisms*. A simple tool like *Strong's Exhaustive Concordance* can assist in their study. It will identify some of the more common ones in its Hebrew and Greek dictionaries.

SOME EXAMPLES OF
SEXUAL EUPHEMISMS
FROM THE BIBLE

Euphemisms for Intercourse

knew (Genesis 4:1)
go in unto (Genesis 38:8)
went in unto (Genesis 16:4)
lie with (Genesis 39:7)
uncover the nakedness (Leviticus 18:12)
spread thy skirt (Ruth 3:9)
touch (I Corinthians 7:1)
due benevolence (I Corinthians 7:3)
come together (I Corinthians 7:5)
the bed (Hebrews 13:4)
uncomely parts (I Corinthians 12:23)[1]
secrets (Deuteronomy 25:11)
stones (Deuteronomy 23:1)
sporting (Genesis 26:8)
grind (Job 31:9-10)
eateth (Proverbs 30:20)

---

1. "Uncomely parts" is *Strong's Greek Lexicon* #809, *askemon*, which Strong says is the origin of #808, *aschemosune*, which he defines as, "by implication, the pudenda [the external genital organs]."

Euphemisms for the Male Sex Organ

mandrakes (Song of Solomon 7:13)
thigh (Genesis 24:2-3)
feet (Isaiah 7:20; Ruth 3:7)
fruit (Song of Solomon 2:3)
loins (I Kings 8:19)
head (Song of Solomon 5:2)

Euphemisms for the Female Sex Organ

garden (Song of Solomon 4:16)
fountain (Proverbs 5:16)
cistern (Proverbs 5:15)
well (Proverbs 5:15)
navel (Song of Solomon 7:2)
mouth (Proverbs 30:20)

Chapter 15

The Gift of Sexuality

For I would that all men were even as I myself. But every man has his proper gift of God, one after this manner, and another after that (I Corinthians 7:7).

Sex is a gift of God to be valued and enjoyed by both men and women. Indeed, it was a husband's duty to see that he met not only the sexual needs of his wife, but also those of a concubine in his house. – David R. Mace, *The Sacred Fire,* Abingdon Press, 1986, p. 32

Human beings are divinely ordained to have sex with one another. God tells the first human beings to have sex. – T.J. Hornsby, *Sex Texts from the Bible,* p. 16

Erotic intimacy is the final answer to God's initial concern that *"it is not good that man should be alone"* (Genesis 2:18) … The first and foremost expression of joy in the Bible is that of the first man when he recognizes his erotic partner and how much she corresponds to him: *"This is now bone of my bone and flesh of my flesh."* – David M. Carr, *The Erotic Word,* Oxford University Press, 2003, p. 34

Paul clearly teaches that sexuality is a GIFT from God. Speaking of one's sexual course and capacity he says, *"Every man has his proper **gift of God,"*** immediately showing the diversity of the divine gift – *"one after this manner, and another after that."*

It is actually amazing where we find this affirmation of sexuality as a *"gift of God."* It is the middle of a passage of Scripture that many find difficult sexually, one that is sometimes used to promote the idea of the spiritual superiority of celibacy. To better appreciate Paul's revelation of sexuality as a *"gift of God,"* it would do the student of Scripture well to square off with the context of I Corinthians chapter 7.

Paul did not have a negative view of sexuality, as some might be led to believe by religious celibate teachings. Even though Paul prefaces his gloriously liberating statement with, *"For I would that all men were even as I myself,"* it must be remembered that this was not always Paul's preference for others. Later he wrote boldly to the other persuasion,

> I will therefore that the younger women marry, bear children, guide the house
> ... (I Timothy 5:14).

THE CONTEXT OF I CORINTHIANS 7

How do we understand these statements from Paul, which are clearly at the opposite ends of the spectrum? The answer will be found in the circumstances of I Corinthians chapter 7. Such a contextual study will confirm that we can accept at full face value Paul's wonderful testament to the origin and nature of sexuality as a *"gift of God"* as divinely revealed to us in :7.

Is one *"manner"* of sexuality (the case at hand – *singleness*[1]) somehow a more spiritual lifestyle? Just what is the context of this chapter? There were serious circumstances (although the particulars are unknown to us) which influenced Paul's specific *"judgment"* (i.e., advice[2]) to the unmarried *at Corinth*.

---

1. It is important to distinguish between Paul's advice regarding *singleness* and a supposed doctrine of "celibacy." Being single and being celibate are two very different things.
2. Some of the things that Paul wrote in response to the Corinthians (7:1) were the *"commandments of the Lord."* These are those things concerning which Paul had a revelation from the Lord.
    Concerning the things about which the Lord had *not* given him specific revelation, he simply applied wisdom and gave his personal *"judgment."* (The word translated *"judgment"* here – *gnome*, *Strong's Greek Lexicon* #1106 – is translated in the *King James Version* as *"advice"* in II Corinthians 8:10). What he speaks regarding his desire for others to follow his singleness as a pattern during *"the present distress"* was a part of this *advice*. He begins the section of personal advice by saying, *"But I speak this by permission and not of commandment"* (I Corinthians 7:6). Notice Paul's language of personal decision making:
    > I speak this by permission ... (:6)
    > I would ... (:7)
    > I say ... (:8)
    > ... Speak I, not the Lord... (:12)
    > ... I have no commandment of the Lord ... (:25)
    > ... I give my judgment ... (:25)
    > I suppose ... (:26)
    > ... This I say ... (:29)
    > ... This I speak ... (:35)

We clearly can see the severe nature of these conditions in the following verses from the same chapter (I Corinthians 7):

> *I suppose therefore that this is good for* **THE PRESENT DISTRESS,** *I say, that it is good for a man so to be* (:26).

> *But this I say, brothers,* **THE TIME IS SHORT:** *it remains, that both they who have wives be as though they had none* (:29).

One could only really surmise what was in Paul's heart and mind as he used the phrases, *"the present distress"* and *"the time is short."* One thing is certain: those to whom he addressed these words – the Corinthian saints – would have understood the serious situation in which they found themselves that sparked these words.

There was a *"present distress"* which caused Paul to believe that the time was *"short."* We do not know what this distress was. It could have been a local situation in Corinth (political, economic, social or religious), or it could have been a distress on a much larger scale. It could even have stemmed from Paul's understanding of the duration and ending of the body of Christ. Perhaps Paul expected the dispensation of grace to come to a quick end with great tribulation in store.[3]

TEMPORARY ADVICE

Whatever the cause of this *"present distress,"* it was of significant magnitude in Paul's mind to cause him to advise the unmarried *at Corinth* to remain so. This was a *temporary* reversal of the natural pattern and plan of God for men to marry:

> *And the LORD God said, "It is not good that the man should be alone; I will make him an help meet for him"* (Genesis 2:18).

We know that this was temporary advice for two reasons.

Paul's words of personal advice to the Corinthian believers were spoken in contrast with the actual instruction that came from the Lord, *"yet not I, but the Lord"* (:10).

Now make no mistake about it: all of this chapter is the inspired Word of God. The *"commandments of the Lord"* are the inspired *instruction* from the Lord; whereas the *"judgment"* of Paul, which he gave without divine revelation, was nonetheless inspired for us so that we may have a pattern of *decision making* when there is not clear revelation from God on a matter.

3. It must be remembered that this is one of Paul's earlier letters, prior to his having received the *full* revelation of the mystery of God. Paul receives this divine knowledge later in his ministry and pens his final letters – thus completing (*"fulfilling"* – i.e., filling full) the Word of God with the pinnacle of progressive revelation committed to his trust (Colossians 1:25).

First, there are the actual words used in I Corinthians 7. They lend themselves to the temporary nature of Paul's instructions. He uses **"present,"** placing a narrow scope on the word *"distress"* – it was a **"present** *distress."* This was not a permanent distress, nor a future distress; but however great it was, it was only a **"present** *distress."* This was the basis of his supposition (*"suppose"*) regarding marriage.

> I **suppose therefore** *that this is good for* THE PRESENT DISTRESS, *I say, that it is good for a man so to be* (:26).

The next word we should notice is the word *"short"* in his phrase *"time is short."* Paul again places a narrow time frame on the scope of his discussion, rather than a broad span of time – something *"short"* – temporary and transient, instead of permanent and lasting.

Second, we know the temporary nature of Paul's *"judgment"* to the believers *at Corinth*, because as we have noted earlier, in a later letter to Timothy he returns to the divine pattern:

> *I will therefore that the younger women marry, bear children, guide the house* … (I Timothy 5:14).

Paul's later instruction was clear: he wanted the younger women to marry. This was a return to the divine pattern of marriage. So, whatever was *"the present distress,"* it had either passed by the time he had written I Timothy, or it was restricted to the region of Corinth the entire time.

That Paul's encouragement of singleness as the *best choice* was related directly to *"the present distress"* can be seen in the fact that he instructs the married to remain so (:10-15). Paul encourages those who are married to carry out their marital ministry toward each other (:3-5). He even encourages those who cannot *"contain"* (:9) to go ahead and marry (:2).

GOD'S GIFT OF SEXUALITY

The *"gift"* of which Paul spoke in :7 is a natural gift in regards to sexuality (and as a result, marriage). I say *natural,* as one might say someone had a "gift of music" or a "gift of art," that it is an inherent part of who they are naturally. Paul's *"gift"* (or his natural inclination) was to be single. These natural sexual desires (or, in this case, the lack of them) were viewed by Paul to have great value (especially in view of *"the present distress"*) (:32-35).

Yet singleness was not the only gift, even during *"the present distress."* There was clearly another *"gift."*

> For I would that all men were even as I myself. But every man has **his** proper gift of God, **one after this manner, and another after that** (I Corinthians 7:7).

Note how Paul says, **"every man** has **his** proper gift of God." The word translated *"his proper"* simply means *"his own"* – **"every man** has HIS OWN gift of God."[4] Every man's *"proper"* gift of sexuality is *"his own"* gift of sexuality – not someone else's!

Each person has their own sexual gift from God. *"Another after that"* gift is the natural gift of sexuality in marriage. I believe that our natural desires (or lack of them) to sexuality and marriage are to be viewed as a *"gift of God."*

Personally, I have the *"another after that"* gift! I have my *"own"* gift from God of sexuality and marriage. I thank God for this gift! I could not even imagine living outside of matrimony – and *for me* it is my *"own"* means to greater service to God! *"But every man has his own gift of God."*

It is a shame that so many saints over the years, and even today, have lived under bondage to some supposed superiority of celibacy based on specific instructions given by Paul to believers nearly two-thousand years ago in a city facing unique circumstances. The saints deserve better Bible teaching than this!

---

4. The word translated *"his proper"* in the *King James Version* in I Corinthians 7:7 is *Strong's Greek Lexicon* #2398, *idios,* and is defined by Strong as "pertaining to self, *i.e.,* one's own; by implication, private or separate." The *King James Version* also translates this word as *"his own"* (Matthew 9:1; 25:14; Mark 15:20; Luke 2:3; 6:44; 10:24; John 1:11, 41, 44; 5:43; 7:18; 8:44; 10:3-4; 13:1; 15:19; 16:32; 19:27; Acts 1:7, 25; 2:6; 4:32; 13:36; 20:28; 28:30; Romans 8:32; 14:4-5; I Corinthians 3:8; 6:18; 7:4, 37; 9:7; 11:21; 15:23, 38; Galatians 6:5; I Timothy 3:4-5; 5:8; II Timothy 1:9; Hebrews 7:27; 9;12; 13:12; James 1:14; II Peter 2:22).

Chapter 16

The Lost Story of the Making of Woman

And the LORD God caused a deep sleep to fall upon Adam, and he slept: and he took one of his ribs, and closed up the flesh instead thereof; And the rib, which the LORD God had taken from man, made He a woman, and brought her unto the man (Genesis 2:21-22).

We know the story well. Or, at least we think we do.

When we read the story of the making of woman in almost all English translations, the true details of the account are veiled from us. It has been almost completely lost due to the mistranslation of the Hebrew word *tsela*.

Is it true that when God made Eve, that He took one of Adam's *"ribs"* to make her?

Is man missing a *"rib"*?

Is man's drive back to the woman … to get his *"rib"* back?

What is the meaning and significance of such a construction?

Tsela is translated as *"rib"* in almost all English translations of the Bible, but is that the true meaning of the word in this passage? What is extremely interesting is that this passage is the only place in Scripture where this Hebrew word is translated as *"rib."* This can be confirmed by any Hebrew concordance. This in itself should raise our concerns.

As A.E. Knoch verifies this,

> The Hebrew word here rendered *"rib,"* though it occurs over forty times, is nowhere else so translated. It is not the Hebrew equivalent of the Chaldee *galag* (Daniel 7:5), the only other word which may be rendered *"rib."*[1]

So why is it that this is the only passage in the Bible where the word *"tsela"* is translated as *"rib"* by translators – especially when the word for "rib" does not even appear in the passage?

I suggest to you a Victorian cover-up. It was something that early English translators were socially and religiously embarrassed to translate, and almost all subsequent translators have followed suit. The translators developed this sort of euphemistic "translation" style when it came to sexually difficult passages.

What was the *"rib"* that was taken from Adam, from which God made Eve? Simply put it was the female sexual organs: labia, clitoris, vagina, cervix, uterus (womb), fallopian tube, and ovaries. *That's* what God took from Adam from which He made Eve.

The *Concordant Literal Version* translates the Hebrew word *tsela* as *"angular organ"* instead of *"rib,"* and has this note on Genesis 2:21:

> Here the female parts of humanity are severed from the male, to build the woman. The breasts of the male are a vestigial reminder that humanity was originally bisexual.

God originally had created Adam with both male and female sexual organs – an hermaphrodite.[2] Even before the record of the creation of Eve we read that *"God*

---

1. A.E. Knoch, *The Building of Woman*, Unsearchable Riches, Vol. XI, No. 6, 1920.
2. Some children are still born "intersexual" (Disorders of Sexual Development – DSD) and are "assigned" their sexuality by "corrective surgery."
   "Ironically since the advancements in surgery have made it possible for intersex conditions to be concealed, many people are not aware of how frequently intersex conditions arise in human beings or that they occur at all." – Alice Domurat Dreger, *Ambiguous Sex,* The Hastings Center Report, May/June 1998, Volume 28, Issue 3, pp. 24-35.
   "Modern surgical techniques help maintain the two-sex system. Today children who are born 'either/ or-neither/both' – a fairly common phenomenon – usually disappear from view because doctors

created He him; male and female" (Genesis 1:27).

Again quoting from Knoch,

> It is a notable fact which is usually overlooked that humanity was *"created male and female"* (Genesis 1:27). The sexes were combined in one individual. Adam was first formed, then Eve. There was an interval between the creation of the man and the building of the woman. *After* the creation of Adam, God planted a garden eastward in Eden. He put the man in the garden to dress it and keep it. He commanded the man as to what he was and was not to eat, and He brought every animal of the field to Adam, who gave them their names.
>
> Let us press the fact, which is repeated in the fifth chapter, that *"In the day that God created man … male and female created He them … and called their name Adam in the day when they were created."* It is evident that the Scriptures are true in a much stricter sense than many suppose, that the woman was taken out of man. Nothing new was *created* when the woman was built. The man permanently lost part of his structure which God removed when He created his helpmeet. In other words, the sexes were separated and Adam retained only masculine functions and Eve was built from the feminine. And do not the facts of the physical world perfectly confirm this interpretation? How could the removal of a rib change Adam from an hermaphrodite to the exclusively masculine structure of his descendants? Such a combination of the sexes is true today of most plants and some worms and mollusks.
>
> It seems most reasonable then, to believe, on the evidence of Scripture as well as nature, that woman was not a separate creation from man, but was built from that part of his original structure which he now lacks.
>
> This is fraught with much beautiful material for reflection. Man, once complete in himself, is now but a part of his original self. The primal perfection can only be attained by the union of the two. They are in very deed one flesh. The One who severed them from one another in that deep sleep which fell upon Adam is the One who yokes them together in holy wedlock.
>
> And is not this the key to our Lord's discourse against divorce? He is very emphatic. "From the *beginning* of creation He makes them male and female."

'correct' them right away with surgery." – Ann Fausto-Sterling, *Sexing the Body: Gender Politics and the Construction of Sexuality,* 2000, New York: Basic Books. According to Ann Fausto-Sterling's research 17 out of 1,000 human births are intersex.

This can refer only to the time when both were included in the one human being Adam. Hence, "*On this account* a man will be leaving his father and mother and will be joined to his wife, and the two will be for one flesh, so that they are no longer two, but one flesh. Then that which God yokes together let no man be severing."[3]

---

3. For further Scriptural details on this subject read Knoch's entire article, Appendix #1.

Chapter 17

The Woman Made for the Man

Neither was the man created for the woman; but the woman for the man (I Corinthians 11:9).

ere is the root of everything sexual. Listen closely to those words. The man was *NOT* created *for* the woman. The woman was created *for* the man. She was made for him; specifically designed and skillfully equipped for him. We know as well, from the account of Genesis chapter two, that she was made *out of* him.

God did not take a *"rib"* from Adam to make Eve. God masterfully took Adam and put him to sleep, performing the first surgery of history. While Adam was *"under,"* God removed his female parts from *"down under."* He sealed Adam's "incision" (*"closed up the flesh instead thereof"*) and then proceeded to make the woman.[1] Every male member of Adam's race bears the mark of this surgery as a reminder. From birth until death: the "surgical scar" is present across the scrotum to the point of the anus.

Man is not missing a *"rib."* Man's drive to the woman is not to get back his *"rib."* Instead, man is driven to regain his missing female parts. His maleness longs for her femaleness. He aches to have back what he has lost. There is a deeply-rooted emptiness within him that only having her back can satisfy.

This is man's true post-op condition, and it is just the way God wants it to be.

---

1. Notice how closely related all the "female" words are to the "male": woMAN, woMEN, feMALE, sHE, HEr, LADy.

Instead of being a hermaphrodite, he is now singularly male; but now he is drawn like a magnet, by divine design, back to his female parts. This is a *godly* drawing. Man did not acquire his drive for the female as a result of his sinful fall, but of his divine construction. This was all in accordance with the Creator's careful blueprint.

God has created the man with the innate *need* of the counterpart, corresponding to his maleness. It is in his reunion with woman that he is humanly complete. He longs for her femininity to be reunited with his masculinity. He pants for her to be returned to him. He needs his receptor back, which corresponds to his male member – a reunion of oneness, his place called "home."

Men have a natural, inherent attraction to *women*. This drawing appeal is God's embedded magnet in *men* for *women*. It is a divinely-designed human magnetism. Man's desire, longing and drive for the woman are indeed godly, for God has specifically engineered him that way.

A man's drive is to become one flesh again with the woman. She is his aim. She is his yearning. She is his hunger. She is his passion. She is his weakness. Without her he is homesick.

Eugene Hillman observes, regarding this drive,

> It comes from the fact that God took woman from man, that they actually were originally *one* flesh. Therefore they must come together again and thus by destiny they belong to each other.[2]

Man and woman, male and female, masculinity and femininity – this is at the very heart of who we are. It is the core of who God has made us. This is not a result of the fall, but of God's wise creation. It is not about sin, it is about fulfillment – fulfillment of divine purpose.

Sexuality is at the very origin of our humanity. Male and female is how we face *every* situation. It is how we view life. It is how our individual worlds are painted. We are *never* divorced from it. Every area of life is affected, influenced and controlled by it. Any attempt to castrate our own personal sexuality from our lives only strikes at the very heart of our being.

Men have sexual thoughts all throughout the day. Any man can attest to this. This

---

2. Eugene Hillman, *Polygamy Reconsidered,* Orbis Books, 1975, p. 154.

is because we are designed by God to do so. To be a man is to be the male sex. So everything is seen, perceived and thought about in maleness. Everything passes through our manhood, through our sexuality. Anything less is emasculation.

Men often have been conditioned to condemn themselves for their sexual thoughts. They are manipulated by religion to feel guilty for being male. This should not be the case. Men become sexually aroused *because* they are men. This is the way they were made by God. This is very natural and godly. This is nothing about which to be ashamed or to feel guilty.

The Bible *never* describes sexuality, or its accompanying desire and arousal as *inherently* sinful. It is therefore *always* godly unless it is used to some *sinful* end. Scripturally, sexual sins are those that defraud others (adultery and rape), confuse family headship (incest), and worship false gods (fornication and going after "strange women").

I will be personally frank with you. I did not always understand these things. Early in my Christian life I was exposed to a moralistic religion that had great appeal and held tremendous sway upon me. It attempted to dominate with a very unnatural perception and censure of my God-given masculinity. After many years of seriously studying the Scriptures I was led to the freedom to be who God made me – a man. I am "horny" because God designed me that way. I didn't come up with the idea. I didn't ask to be made this way. This is not a complaint; it's just the facts of life and nature. I will not stand one day before God to be judged for the sex-drive and appeal for women that He gave me. Neither will I stand before God to be condemned for their godly use.

Chapter 18

The History of Sex and Religion

There is often a fear or uneasiness of talking about sexuality and sexual conduct. Why is this? What is the source of this apprehension for something that is so basic to who we are?

Why is the subject so delicate and forbidding for adults that they are uncomfortable discussing it with their children?

We believe that what is known as Gnosticism,[1] which has permeated much of Christendom's attitude throughout its history, is responsible for a great deal of the sexual negativity and unwholesomeness of our culture.

WHERE IT ALL STARTED

What the modern world still understands by "sin" stems **not** from the teaching of Jesus of Nazareth, or from the tablets handed down from Sinai, but from the early sexual vicissitudes of a handful of men who lived in the twilight days of imperial Rome.[2]

Gnosticism had an ancient history and has continued in many forms up to the present time … Its influence in sexual theory has been one of the most negative influences within the church … There are many forms of Gnostic belief. In the Protestant Church it helped form much of the point-of-view of Puritanism, and

---

1. Gnosticism was a syncretistic religious system made up of Oriental theosophy and Greek philosophy. Its chief tenet was that "matter" is evil and that "spirit" is good … Gnosticism reached the peak of its power around A.D. 150. (Roy Gingrich, *The History of the Church*, Riverside Press, 1980, p. 16.)
2. Reay Tannahill, *Sex in History*, Scarbough House, 1992, p. 138.

in the Roman Catholic Church it dominated the attitude of Jansenism that influenced the training of many men and women's Catholic religious orders. In the Old Testament we find almost none of this negativity toward sexuality.[3]

Gnosticism makes its full impact on the Christian Church in the second century where it was a totally pervasive element in the intellectual climate.

It isn't until St. Augustine[4] of Hippo in the late fourth century that we find the Gnostic viewpoint about sexuality predominating. Early in the Church's life a conflict arose about the nature of evil that wasn't resolved until the end of the fourth century. The mainline Christians accepted the Old Testament as Scripture and believed that God revealed there was ultimate spiritual reality. Along with the Hebrews they believed that the physical world was an expression of the Divine, the direct creation of God, and therefore good. The Gnostic attitude toward creation on the other hand sprang out of Persian thinking that saw two equal and opposite divine creative forces – the light and the dark. In the Persian view both the light and the dark were present in the spiritual world and in nature. The main purpose of human morality and religion was to support the forces of light and so enable them to conquer darkness and bring salvation to the universe.[5]

CHANGING VIEWS

Ultimately, however, a perversion of this Persian viewpoint developed and became a seductive Christian heresy. The dark force became equated with matter, with physicality and with the God of the Old Testament, while the light force became equated with spirit, spirituality, asceticism and Jesus Christ. In Gnosticism, matter was seen as ugly, irredeemable and evil. The creation of human beings in this point of view was an imprisoning of pure and holy spirit in vile matter. If we believe that spiritual reality is a realm of bliss, harmony and ecstasy (what the Gnostic called the *pleroma*) then the mingling of spirit and matter becomes a cosmic catastrophe rather than purposeful, orderly and good.

In the myth of Gnosticism, such a cosmic catastrophe did occur; the realm of blissful spirit exploded and little fragments of spirit became imbedded in the earth where they became human beings. In the midst of such a catastrophe,

3. Morton and Barbara Kelsey, *Sacrament of Sexuality: The Spirituality and Psychology of Sex*, Amity House, 1986.
4. "Augustine … crowned Western theology with a negativity toward sex." Raymond J. Lawrence, Jr., *The Poisoning of Eros: Sexual Values in Conflict*, Augustine Moore Press, 1989, p. 2.
5. Frank Bottomley, *Attitudes to the Body in Western Christendom*, Lepus Books, 1979, p. 184, note 9.

how is salvation achieved? Through asceticism, by eliminating any attachment to the world of physical reality and by getting rid of emotional involvement and physical pleasure. However, there is something far worse than failing to be detached: bringing more soul or spirit into the world of matter thus becomes the ultimate evil, conception becomes the worse possible human act. Carrying this idea to its logical conclusion, one extreme Gnostic sect, the Manichaeans, taught that intercourse with pre-adolescent girls was not ultimately evil because pregnancy was not possible. Even the Roman Emperors were shocked by this idea and outlawed the sect.

Gradually the idea developed within this sect that anything to do with conception, or copulation, or sexuality, or genital organs was evil or ugly. St. Augustine was a fringe member of the Manichaean sect for nine years and although he eventually disengaged himself intellectually, he never entirely disengaged himself emotionally. His little book "The Good of Marriage" has some passages on marriage that are well nigh unbelievable. Even normal sexual intercourse within marriage can be venial sin; the quicker married people abstain from all sexual relations the better for their souls.[6]

THE NEW PLATONISM

The first Platonic philosopher who joined the Christians was Justin Martyr ... followed by Clement of Alexandria, A.D. 192, who had a school in the city called the Catechetic School, which attempted to harmonize the philosophy of Plato with the materialism of the Gnostics by means of the common medium of Christianity. This scheme was called the New Platonism; and a long contest prevailed between the followers of this system and the advocates for gospel simplicity.[7]

WORSE THAN BARBARIC PERSECUTION

Under the influences of Greek Gnostic thinking and Roman laws, the principles of Christianity suffered worse than it did through the centuries of barbaric persecution ... It was during the Dark Ages of Christianity that the celibates and Gnostics infused their ideologies into the doctrines of Christ.[8]

6. Kelsey, *Op. Cit.*

7. James Campbell, *A History and Philosophy of Marriage*, Patriarch Publishing House, 2007, p. 71.

8. Ogden Kraut, *Polygamy in the Bible*, Pioneer Publishing, 1983.

To this C.S. Lewis agreed:

> Of all tyrannies a tyranny sincerely exercised for the good of its victims may be the most oppressive. It may be better to live under robber barons than under omnipotent moral busybodies. The robber baron's cruelty may sometimes sleep, his cupidity may at some point be satiated; but those who torment us for own good will torment us without end, for they do so with the approval of their own conscience.[9]

THE "EARLY CHURCH'S" TEACHINGS ABOUT SEX

A noticeable feature of Patristic thought, particularly in the West, is the growing suspicion (indeed, it amounts to fear) of sex, which attains extravagant, even ridiculous proportions in the writings of Tertullian and Jerome, and relapses into a more moderate negative attitude in those of Augustine, Ambrose and Gregory the Great ...

The significance of sex in the personal life of the individual was never appreciated, nor was sexual intercourse seen to possess any meaning or even importance in the experience of husband and wife as "one flesh," save for the purpose of procreation.

Thus early Christianity left to succeeding ages an unbalanced conception of sex and sexual intercourse, and an entirely mistaken view of sexual pleasure ... This failure to understand sex contributed to the exaltation of celibacy ...[10]

GREEK TRADITION

From the outset, Christianity has depicted sex as a dangerous, chaotic, anti-spiritual force. In this, the early Christians were influenced by anti-sexual elements of Greek tradition.[11]

---

9. C.S. Lewis, *The Humanitarian Theory of Punishment*, June 1953.
10. Derrick Sherwin Bailey, *The Mystery of Love and Marriage.*
11. David M. Carr, *The Erotic Word,* Oxford University Press, 2003, p. 5.

ORIGEN (185-254)

Origen … was a kind of Christian Gnostic.[12]

Origen reckoned conjugal intercourse inconsistent with the presence of the Holy Spirit.[13]

Origen, a still more learned and more voluminous writer, and a very eloquent preacher, embraced the Gnostic errors when a young man, and carried his principles of subduing the passions of the body to such an extent, that he made a eunuch of himself.[14]

Origen harbored such a strong distaste for physical love that he actively discouraged sexual intercourse between husbands and wives. This abhorrence of anything sexual led him to campaign against keeping the Song of Solomon in the collection of inspired writings … He refused to believe that God inspired a book which recommended married lovemaking. … As the only alternative left for him … Origen mutilated God's word by devising an allegory of Christ and the church. Since most of the religious leaders of Catholicism at that time shared Origen's views of prudery, they embraced his allegory.

Then in 533 A.D. the Catholic church denounced all literal interpretations of the book. As a result, the allegorical theory "reigned supreme" for the next thousand years among Christian interpreters. (*The International Standard Bible Encyclopedia,* Vol. V, p. 2832; *c.f.* Albert Reville, *The Song of Songs,* page 6).[15]

MISSIONARY POSITION

The so-called "missionary position" was not invented by missionaries, but by the 2nd century Greek philosopher and dream interpreter, Artemidorus. He proposed the face-to-face man-on-top position as the only proper one, and that oral eroticism was "an awful act."[16]

---

12. Frank Bottomley, *Attitudes To The Body In Western Christendom,* Lepus Books, 1979, p. 73.
13. Justin D. Fulton, *Why Priests Should Wed,* Evangelist L.J. King, Toledo, Ohio, 1913, p. 59.
14. Campbell, *Op. Cit.*
15. P.R. Dawson, *Marriage: A Taste of Heaven,* Gospel Themes Press, 1995.
16. Lawrence, *Op. Cit.,* p. 12.

POPE GREGORY THE GREAT (540-604)

Pope Gregory the Great said that married people should not receive communion after intercourse unless they had first done penance. Later writers, including the standard [Catholic] theological authors of the twelfth century, argued that passion actually transmitted original sin by corrupting the seed with its heat.[17]

Speaking of the attitude toward marital sex, Gardelia, regarding the obligation of Catholics at the Fourth Lateran Council in 1215, states that,

Sexual pleasure with one's spouse remained a venial sin. Venial sin did not destroy the saving work of God's grace in the soul, as mortal sin would; but taking pleasure even in marital sex weakened and stained the soul and so required that the sinner do penance on earth or after death. ...

Pope Gregory the Great, for example, had forbidden sex during nursing lest the milk be spoiled or contaminated ... many had sought to limit to a face-to-face position with the man on top, because they believed that any other posture had a contraceptive effect.[18]

Oral sex ranked as "a more horrible kind of sodomy" than anal intercourse, and entailed more horrible possibilities of disease.[19]

CANONICAL PROHIBITATIONS

In 729 St. Ecgbert, Archbishop of York, composed a book of canonical writings. ...

A husband having intercourse with a menstruating wife is due for forty days [of fasting]. ...

In some Penitentials a fast of as much as seven years is prescribed for a husband who copulates with his wife "like a dog." For this posture was considered to provide an *excessive* amount of pleasure for the partners. But

---

17. Peter Gardelia, *Innocent Ecstasy,* Oxford University Press, 1985, p. 11, citing Augustine, *On Marriage and Concupiscence*, 2.53-54, 59; also, *The City of God*, Book XIV, chapters 16-24, and John T. Noonan, Jr., *Contraception: A History of Its Treatment by Catholic Theologians and Canonists* (Cambridge: Harvard University Press, 1965), pp. 57ff.

18. *Ibid.,* p. 11, 13.

19. *Ibid.,* p. 37, citing Adolphe Tanquerey, *Synopsis Theologiae Moralis et Pastoralis*, 7th ed. (Rome, 1920), Volume II, Supplementum, paragraph 28.

if he actually commits sodomy upon her he is to fast for the rest of his life and suffer excommunication. Conjugal relations on a Sunday, even after dark, are punished by three day's fasting. Legitimate sexual intercourse is also to be omitted for forty days before Easter, seven days before Whitsun and fourteen days before Christmas.

Habitual masturbation carried three years [fasting] ... A single act of masturbation is punished on one page by four meatless days. Yet elsewhere, if the offender is a young boy he gets a month, if a man forty days.

Confessors were instructed in later manuals to question very closely penitents who admitted sexual misbehavior ...

Bishop Burchard of Worms (d. 1025) gives some interesting examples of such interrogations, along a particular line of enquiry, in a *Decretum* which also includes the appropriate penalties for affirmative replies.

"Have you done," he is to repeat inexorably, "what certain women are wont to do, sitting upon the aforesaid instrument or some other device of similar construction, and thus committing fornication upon yourself in solitude?"

If the penitent confesses to having arranged a private indulgence of her prudence in this way she is to fast for one year.

The Bishop leaves no legal loophole for evasion in this matter. For he adds: "Any woman using any fornicating instrument whatever, either alone or in company with another woman, must fast for three years, the first on bread and water only."[20]

Chaste Marriages

"Chaste marriages" were a feature of the period from the second to the tenth Christian centuries. An Anglo-Saxon queen was actually canonized for refusing intercourse with her husband.[21]

Nuns Disfigured

Nuns proved their contempt for the natural interests of young women by scarring

---

20. James Cleugh, *Love Locked Out,* Tandem Books, 1967, pp. 255, 257, 258, 259, 260.
21. *Ibid.,*p. 10.

their faces and cutting off their breasts as well as their hair. An Alexandrian nun actually blinded herself after being told by a visitor that she had beautiful eyes.[22]

PETER ABELARD (1079-1142)

The thousand-year period between Augustine and Luther (the Middle Ages) was a time of the implementation and solidification of Augustinian valorization of sexuality.

[Peter Abelard] challenged the church's established view that sexual pleasure was to be avoided. He wrote in *Ethics 3*, "If to lie with a wife or even to eat delicious food has been allowed us since the first day of our creation which was lived in paradise without sin, who will accuse us of sin in this if we do not exceed the limits of the concession?" He brilliantly mocks the accepted teaching of his day: "... they say ... marital intercourse ... should be performed wholly without pleasure. But assuredly, if this is so, they are allowed to be done in a way in which they cannot be done at all and it was an unreasonable permission which allowed them to be done in a way which it is certain that they cannot be done." (*Peter Abelard's Ethics*, Oxford: Clarendon Press, 1971, p. 21)

The Pope declared Abelard a heretic, ordered his books burned and ... in death, as in life, Abelard was not allowed to rest. His remains were interred seven times before they were finally left in peace.[23]

THOMAS AQUINAS (1225-1274)

When Thomas Aquinas drew up a hierarchy of sexual sins, he classified masturbation as a more serious sin than fornications between consenting partners, seduction of a virgin, or adultery. Masturbation was more sinful because it omitted the object created by God for the sexual drive, the genital organ of the opposite sex. Masturbation was one of the "unnatural vices," all of which were more sinful than illicit copulation because they violated the law of nature.[24]

JOHN CALVIN (1509-1564)

It is said that the French reformer, John Calvin was particularly preoccupied with adultery, and made references to it in almost every matter he discussed. G.

---

22. *Ibid.*, p. 274.
23. Lawrence, *Op. Cit.*, p. 134, 151, 152.
24. Gardelia, *Op. Cit.*, page 10, citing Thomas Aquinas, *Summa Theologiae*, 2-2.154.12.

Rattray Taylor, commenting on this characteristic in Sex in History, generalizes that "Since repression always stimulates what it sets out to repress, one is not surprised to learn that his (Calvin's) sister-in-law was taken in adultery in 1557 and that his daughter suffered a like fate five years later."[25]

Marriage, for example, was not ever universally required to legitimize sexual activity even in western Christian society. It was not until the Council of Trent in 1565, that the Church declared that a Christian ceremony was necessary in order to have a valid marriage.[26]

Prudish Calvinist

The European Calvinists believed that "the life of sex is not to be used for enjoyment, but for the deliberate procreation of Children."[27]

MODERN MORAL CRUSADERS

Listening to many of the moralists preach and crusade for their legalistic sexual bondage to be imposed upon others, one would think that some of the greatest sins of the Bible would surely be sexual in nature. This is because religion actually has a negative obsession with sexuality. Let us consult the Scriptures themselves to see the six sins that God hates, the seven that are an abomination unto Him.

SIX THINGS GOD HATES:
SEVEN THINGS THAT ARE ABOMINATIONS TO HIM

These six things does the LORD hate: yea, seven are an abomination to Him: a proud look, a lying tongue, and hands that shed innocent blood, a heart that devises wicked imaginations, feet that are swift in running to mischief, a false witness that speaks lies, and he who sows discord among brothers (Proverbs 6:16-19).

There they are. Let's count them:

(1) *a proud look*
(2) *a lying tongue*

25. G. Rattray Taylor, *Sex in History: The Story of Society's Changing Attitudes to Sex Throughout the Ages,*.New York: The Vanguard Press, Inc., 1970, p. 164.

26. John Shelby Spong, *Living in Sin,* San Franscisco: Harper and Roe, 1988, p. 65.

27. Ernst Troeltsch, *The Social Teachings of the Christian Churches,* II, trans. Olive Wyon, Allen & Unwin, 1931, p. 809.

(3) *hands that shed innocent blood*
(4) *a heart that devises wicked imaginations*
(5) *feet that are swift in running to mischief*
(6) *a false witness that speaks lies*
(7) *he who sows discord among brothers*

Now, did you notice anything interesting about this list? Is something strikingly absent?

There's not a sexual sin in the bunch!

In fact some of these sins are actually very prominent in moralistic, religious circles! Specifically look at the first and the last from the list – *"a proud look,"* and *"sowing discord among the brothers."* These are what God hates.

Famed author C.S. Lewis wrote,

> If anyone thinks that Christians regard unchastity as the supreme vice, he is quite wrong. The sins of the flesh are bad, but they are the least bad of all sins. All the worst pleasures are purely spiritual: the pleasure of putting other people in the wrong, of bossing and patronizing and spoiling sport, and backbiting; the pleasures of power, of hatred.[28]

E.W. Bullinger noted that,

> The history of Genesis 3 is intended to teach us the fact that Satan's sphere of activities is in the **religious** sphere, and not the spheres of crime or **immorality** … We are not to look for Satan's activities today in the newspaper press, or the police courts; but in the pulpit, and in professors' chairs.[29]

No wonder that when Christ came He was much more at home with *"publicans and sinners"* (Matthew 9:10-11; 11:19; Mark 2:15-16; Luke 5:30; 7:34, 39; 15:1) and *"harlots"* (Luke 7) than with the religious denominations of the Pharisees and Sadducees! They will, in fact, precede the religious in entering the Kingdom of God (Matthew 2:31-32)!

Religious moralists have taken the wonderful gift of human beauty and sexuality and made it something dirty and sinful. Much is at stake here regarding truth. We

28. C.S. Lewis (1898-1963), *Mere Christianity,* Book III, Christian Behavior (chapter 5).
29. E.W. Bullinger, *The Companion Bible,* Appendix 19.

must all decide whether we will continue the shameful sham that has kept people in religious bondage for too long, or if we will live and teach freedom's truth in genuine love, grace and liberty.

> *And that because of false brothers unawares brought in, who came in privately to spy out our liberty which we have in Christ Jesus, that they might bring us into bondage: To whom we gave place by subjection, no, not for an hour; that the truth of the gospel might continue with you* (Galatians 2:4-5).

Chapter 19

Martin Luther and Sexuality

Who loves not wine, women, and song remains a fool his whole life long.[1] – Martin Luther

THE FORGOTTEN LUTHER

The *real* Martin Luther has sadly been veiled from most modern Protestants. This truly amazing and colorful reformer was more radical in his views and life than many have been allowed to know. The area of sexuality is no exception.

Luther was outrageously earthy. Who else in the history of religion would have had the audacity and candor to locate his experience of enlightenment, or conversion, at the time and place of tending to the needs of his bowels? In the Wittenberg monastery toilet Luther was reflecting on the justice of God and the words of Paul, *"the just shall live by faith,"* particularly in the context of his own inner urgency to be right. …

No one in all ecclesiastical history consistently reveals himself to be more body affirming and more human … Luther's candor about the context of his enlightenment in the monastery toilet is only the beginning.[2]

Some of Luther's thoughts on marriage sound radical to many today. Certainly one is not likely to hear them proclaimed from the bashful Protestant pulpit, where sound and fury generally signify nothing very much.[3]

---

1. Raymond J. Lawrence, Jr., *The Poisoning of Eros: Sexual Values in Conflict,* Augustine Moore Press, 1989, p. 2.
2. *Ibid*, p. 171, 176.
3. Richard Marius, *Luther,* Lippincott, 1974, p. 132.

THE SEX-DEVIL INCARNATE

Martin Luther was regarded by his enemies while he lived, and still more after his death, as the sex-devil incarnate.[4]

PLAYFUL AND JOYFUL ATTITUDE
TOWARD LIFE AND SEXUALITY

Luther was an energetic and spontaneous character and was obviously very little concerned that everything he said be consistent. He was never very far removed from a joyful, playful, and even mischievous attitude toward his own sexuality. This playful and joyful approach to things sexual was congruent with his attitude toward life generally. The devil is the one, according to Luther, who fills the world with a "sour spirit," making our "days stretch out and appear salt-less." To counter the devil we must "get up, seek company, start to dance and sing, to play cards and make music. For the devil cannot stand joy."[5] Luther was often playfully erotic and scatological in his conversation. He was almost embarrassingly fond of associating the Pope and the Roman Catholic clergy with things excremental. When a cardinal lets wind, he said, we Germans are supposed to believe a new article of faith is born. Of course, Luther was more than just playful, since the Roman system of salvation was in his vision a work of rationalization and self-justification, and therefore profoundly excremental.

Much of Luther's playfulness was phallic too. When a visiting Waldensian minister named Lawrence shared with Luther his regret at having castrated himself as a youth, Luther replied, "For my part I'd rather have two pair added than one pair cut off."[6] In a letter to his friend Justice Jonas, Luther reveals similar playfulness with sexual innuendo, "My Katie cordially and reverently greets you and all your family. But hold a minute; if my wife greets you, I in turn greet your wife. What is sauce for the goose is sauce for the gander."[7] Luther's phallic playfulness even tested the boundaries of reverence in ways that no doubt horrified the pious then as it still does today ...

Six months after his marriage, Luther wrote to his friend Georg Spalatin, who

4. Richard Lewinsohn, translated by Alexander Mayce, *A History of Sexual Customs*, Harper & Brothers, 1958, p. 176.

5. Heiko A. Oberman, "Luther and the Devil," Lutheran Theological Seminary Bulletin, Winter 1989, p. 10.

6. *Luther's Works*, Vol. 54, p. 177. Theodore G. Tappert & Helmut T. Lahmann eds., Philadelphia: Fortress Press, 1967.

7. John M. Todd, *Luther*, New York: Crossroad, 1982, pp. 342-3.

was about to marry a woman, also named Katie. Luther expressed his regrets at not being able to travel to his friend's wedding, the hazards of the route being too great. So he wrote,

> I will calculate how long it will take my courier to reach you. The very night you receive this letter, you penetrate your lovely Katie, and I will penetrate mine. Thus we will be united in love.

Even at death's door Luther remained playfully perverse and affirming of his sexuality. As a very sick man, perhaps with congestive heart failure, he traveled to Eisleben ... a journey from which he was to return in a coffin. On the outgoing leg of the trip he wrote his beloved Katie that he had recovered from his illness and "now suffer merely from the resistance of the beautiful ladies ..."[8] Luther is unique in Christian history as a theologian who was both aware of and candid about his own polymorphous sexual energy. Luther was so unambiguously affirming of sex and so personally comfortable in that affirmation that intellectual and theological development in the West has not found a way yet to integrate him. Luther has remained too radical in his sexual values even for most of his own followers in the Reformation tradition.[9]

RELIGIOUS CHASTITY

He came to be contemptuous of [religious] chastity vows ... "Nature does not cease to do its work when there is voluntary chastity ... To put it bluntly, seed ... if it does not flow into the flesh will flow into the nightshirt."[10]

NUDITY & CREATION

Luther's understanding of sex [was] as a fact of creation and therefore good ... His commentary on Genesis contributed ... the conviction that ... nudity was no cause for shame ... The strong naturalism inherited in the creation story of the Old Testament was inescapable for Luther ... Luther did not share the Catholic admiration for the contemplative life and he was not alarmed by the disruption of reason involved in orgasm ...[11]

8. Jonas, Coelius, et al., *The Last Days of Luther,* translated and annotated by Martin Ebon, New York: Doubleday, 1970, p. 21.

9. Lawrence, *Op. Cit.,* p. 179-181.

10. *Ibid,,* p. 176.

11. William Graham Cole, *Sex in Christianity and Psychoanalysis,* Oxford University Press, 1955, p. 106.

THE NEED OF SEX

Luther was convinced that some sort of sex life is essential to all men ... Luther's realism was such that he refused to content himself with pious exhortations to men to contain themselves. He knew human nature and he realized that for some men this is literally impossible.[12]

POEM FOR THE MARRIED

Luther in his later years never hesitated to speak openly on sexual questions. He thought this neither immodest nor indiscreet, even when dealing with details which today are regarded as falling within the doctor's province. Hence his famous advice to married couples:

> *A week two*
> *Is the woman's due.*
> *Harms neither me nor you,*
> *Makes in a year, twice fifty-two.*

It makes the "two" sort of a minimum which the wife has a right to expect. ... Had Luther married at twenty-two, instead of forty-two,[13] his rule for marriage might have run differently. In any case, he saw in marital intercourse both a right and a duty for both parties; the woman too, was entitled to it.[14]

MONOGAMY

Luther's conversations at mealtime with his family and friends were recorded for posterity by some of his followers and published as *Table Talk*. On one occasion Luther ventured the opinion at supper that the time would come again when a man will take more than one wife, as he had in patriarchal times.[15]

In at least two complex pastoral counseling cases Luther further demonstrated his lack of commitment to strict monogamy. In one case a woman presented herself as married to a man who was impotent. She wanted to have children and felt herself personally unable to remain sexually continent ... Luther

12. *Ibid.*, pp. 116-117.
13. "He [Luther] was forty-two years of age at his marriage ... while Katherine was twenty-seven." *Ibid.*, p. 105.
14. Richard Lewinsohn, translated by Alexander Mayce, *A History of Sexual Customs*, Harper & Brothers, 1958, p. 177.
15. Lawrence, *Op. Cit.*, p. 180.

recommended that the woman seek her husband's consent for her to take a lover, preferably her husband's brother. Luther was undoubtedly thinking of the Jewish levirate law here. He further advised that any such liaison be kept secret so as not to cause scandal, and that any children issuing from such a liaison be ascribed to her husband.[16]

It was Luther's belief that "If she does this ... she is not involved in sin."[17]

Luther's pastoral direction in this case would not have been understood to be as radical in his day as it would be today, since both Westphalian and Saxon common law prescribed that a man who could not perform his conjugal duty was required to seek satisfaction for his wife through a neighbor.[18]

In a similar case Luther was consulted by a man whose wife ... was unable to fulfill her marital obligation. The man felt himself unable to sustain the burden of chastity, and asked for Luther's advice. Luther replied that ... [he should] take a second wife. Luther ... exhorted him to provide sufficiently for his first wife and not abandon her.[19]

Luther insisted that whatsoever was not specifically forbidden by Scripture was optional for the Christian, and not only is there no biblical ban on polygamy, there are positive examples of it in the patriarchs. In January of 1521 ... Luther had written to a friend whose marital life was wholly asexual owing to the illness of his wife and who had been asked whether he might take a second wife ... Luther had responded that he could raise no objection if a man wished to take several wives, since Holy Scripture does not forbid it.[20]

In fact, the three leading figures of the German reformation, Luther, Melanchthon and Bucer, signed the *Wittenberg Deliberation* which was mostly taken up with an examination of the Biblical authority for polygamy. They jointly gave their public blessing to Philip the Magnanimous of Hesse to marry a second wife. Luther contended that polygamy is not wrong in itself, and definitely preferable to divorce. This was a position that he never diverged from.[21]

16. *Luther's Works,* Vol. 36, Word and Sacrament II, Wentz & Lehmann, eds., Philadelphia: Fortress Press, 1967, p. 103.

17. Cole, *Op. Cit.,* p. 116.

18. *Ibid.,* p. 103.

19. Lawrence, *Op. Cit.,* p. 178.

20. Cole, *Op. Cit.,* pp. 116-117.

21. John Cairncross, *After Polygamy Was Made A Sin: The Social History of Christian Polygamy,* 1974, London: Rouledge & Kegan Paul, pp. 33, 36, 49-50.

Luther wrote, "I confess, indeed, I cannot forbid anyone who wishes to marry several wives, nor is that against Holy Scriptures ..."[22]

THE USE OF THE MAID

His [Luther's] lusty realism asserted itself again on behalf of those whose sex life in marriage was, due to no fault of theirs, nonexistent. His remarks in this connection became well-known, a scandal to many: "If the wife refuses, let the maid come." Luther could not bring himself to condemn a man who dealt with the frigidity of a wife's refusing to render the conjugal debt by ... taking unto himself a more compliant partner.[23]

LUTHER AND
THOMAS MORE (of England)

Luther had for the first half of his life suppressed his sexual desires in monastic life. In the later half he enthusiastically reversed himself to affirm his polymorphous sexual desires as gifts of God ... When Luther married a nun in 1522, More was undoubtedly aghast. From then on his antipathy of Luther and his teachings was fueled with hot indignation. Canon and civil law characterized the marriage of a priest and a nun as incest, punishable by death. To the bitter end More expressed his contempt for this "incestuous" relationship in the most vitriolic terms. The relish with which More burned so many Protestants at the stake, was perhaps in part displaced rage he felt toward Luther whom he could not reach.

Luther's marriage to Katie, the sexual union of the priest/monk and nun, inspired many others in its clear affirmation of sex. However, it horrified many others in ways that his challenge to the authority of the church might never have done. Not only had Luther married a nun, but he had done so with zest. He relished the thought that the pope and his stalwarts were so much more thoroughly horrified by his marriage than they would have been had he married a laywoman. Pope Adrian VI warned rulers in the West to beware "the filthy German Mohammed" who is loose in their midst, and who grants men permission to have many wives.[24, 25]

---

22. Robert Hitchens, *Multiple Marriage: A Study of Polygamy in Light of the Bible,* Elkton, MD, Doulos, 1987, p. 64.
23. Cole, *Op. Cit.,* p. 116.
24. William H. Lazareth, *Luther and the Christian Home,* Philadelphia: Muhlenberg Press, p. 192.
25. Lawrence, *Op. Cit.,* pp. 191-192.

Chapter 20

God's Figurative Language

These six things does the LORD hate: yea, seven are an abomination unto Him: a proud look, a lying tongue, and hands that shed innocent blood, a heart that devises wicked imaginations, feet that are swift in running to mischief, a false witness that speaks lies, and he who sows discord among brothers (Proverbs 6:16-19).

eligion has an obsession with sex – a *negative* obsession.

As we have already considered, there is not a single sexual sin in the list of six sins that God hates, the seven that are an abomination to Him!

Read the list in our text again! Take a closer look and get a better, fresher view of God! This view of God is what made Jesus Christ a friend of publicans and sinners, and an enemy of the pharisaical religious system. They too were obsessed with the evil of sexual issues. Reread the Gospels. Watch their reaction in the face of adultery, or prostitution, for example. Then look again and notice Christ's reaction.

The extreme moralists believe that the whole arena of sexual topics is off limits *even* for discussion. For them it is indecent for adults to discuss the details of God honoring sexual relationships, let alone sinful sexual activity.

This is not true with the God of the Bible. Not only is He *not* ashamed to record erotic material about godly sex, He also has no scruples when it comes to describing the sinful use of sex.

Much of what the Bible has to say about sex would be considered vulgar by many religionists if it was in any other book. In fact, it would not be out of character for the moralist to attempt to boycott such material for censorship from public schools and libraries. Yet at the same time they want the Bible to be in both.

We already have seen a few of the many passages where God presents godly sex in a detailed and erotic way.

If that type of discussion is not shocking enough, we will now look at God's descriptions of sinful sexual activity.

We will take a passage from Ezekiel as our example. In this passage God metaphorically describes Jerusalem's unfaithfulness to Him as *"whoredoms."* He is very sexually graphic in the process.

Do not simply glance or skim over it. Give it a thoughtful reading.

> *Son of man, there were two women, the daughters of one mother: And they committed whoredoms in Egypt; they committed whoredoms in their youth: there were their breasts pressed, and there they bruised the teats of their virginity. And the names of them were Aholah the elder, and Aholibah her sister: and they were mine, and they bare sons and daughters. Thus were their names; Samaria is Aholah, and Jerusalem Aholibah. And Aholah played the harlot when she was mine; and she doted on her lovers, on the Assyrians her neighbors, Which were clothed with blue, captains and rulers, all of them desirable young men, horsemen riding upon horses. Thus she committed her whoredoms with them, with all them who were the chosen men of Assyria, and with all on whom she doted: with all their idols she defiled herself. Neither left she her whoredoms brought from Egypt: for in her youth they lay with her, and they bruised the breasts of her virginity, and poured their whoredom upon her. Wherefore I have delivered her into the hand of her lovers, into the hand of the Assyrians, upon whom she doted. These discovered her nakedness: they took her sons and her daughters, and slew her with the sword: and she became famous among women; for they had executed judgment upon her. And when her sister Aholibah saw this,*

she was more corrupt in her inordinate love than she, and in her whoredoms more than her sister in her whoredoms. She doted upon the Assyrians her neighbors, captains and rulers clothed most gorgeously, horsemen riding upon horses, all of them desirable young men. Then I saw that she was defiled, that they took both one way, And that she increased her whoredoms: for when she saw men portrayed upon the wall, the images of the Chaldeans portrayed with vermilion, Girded with girdles upon their loins, exceeding in dyed attire upon their heads, all of them princes to look to, after the manner of the Babylonians of Chaldea, the land of their nativity: And as soon as she saw them with her eyes, she doted upon them, and sent messengers unto them into Chaldea. And the Babylonians came to her into the bed of love, and they defiled her with their whoredom, and she was polluted with them, and her mind was alienated from them. So she discovered her whoredoms, and discovered her nakedness: then my mind was alienated from her, like as my mind was alienated from her sister. Yet she multiplied her whoredoms, in calling to remembrance the days of her youth, wherein she had played the harlot in the land of Egypt. For she doted upon their paramours, whose flesh is as the flesh of asses, and whose issue is like the issue of horses. Thus you called to remembrance the lewdness of your youth, in bruising your teats by the Egyptians for the paps of your youth (Ezekiel 23:2-21 – King James Version).

Now, it is quite possible that you missed the full impact of this passage. One needs to remember, when reading a passage such as this, that the *King James Version* translators were under the enormous power of the religious sexual ethic of their day.

Reading 17th century English, where the translators deal awkwardly with sexual issues, makes the clear language of the Hebrew quite obscure. Still, we were able to see a rather graphic picture nonetheless.

Let's take a closer look at two of the strong-language verses from this passage. Below we will again put the *KJV* translation of :20-21, and then we will quote them from two modern translations, to help us see what we may have missed.

King James Version

For she doted upon their paramours, whose flesh is as the flesh of asses, and whose issue is like the issue of horses. Thus you called to remembrance the lewdness of your youth, in bruising your teats by the Egyptians for the paps of your youth.

New International Version

There she lusted after her lovers, whose genitals were like those of donkeys and whose emission was like that of horses. So you longed for the lewdness of your youth, when in Egypt your bosom was caressed and your young breasts fondled.

God's Word Translation

She lusted after her lovers, whose genitals were like those of donkeys and whose semen was like that of horses. So she longed to do the sinful things she did when she was young in Egypt, when young men caressed and fondled her breasts.

These modern translations will reflect a social change since 1611 that has allowed for a more straightforward translation of the Hebrew into English.

After having read these verses from modern translations, we will now take the time to study four words from these verses for ourselves. We will find out the definition of these Hebrew words:[1]

DOTED – "to love (sensually)"[2]

PARAMOURS – "a concubine (male or female)"[3]

FLESH – "(by euphemism) the pudenda of a man"[4]

---

1. The issue in these various translations, will be just that – translation. The Hebrew texts will *not* be at issue.
2. *Strong's Hebrew Lexicon* #5689, `agab (aw-gab') a primitive root; to breathe after, *i.e.,* to love (sensually):-- dote, lover.
3. *Young's Analytical Concordance to the Bible.*
4. *Strong's Hebrew Lexicon* #1320, *basar* (baw-sawr'), from 1319; flesh (from its freshness); by extension, body, person; also (by euphem.) the pudenda of a man: -- body, (fat, lean) flesh(-ed), kin, (man-)kind, + nakedness, self, skin.

ISSUE – "a gushing of fluid (semen)"[5] "emission of seed"[6]

God says that she was rather taken by her lovers' well-endowed genitals and their large ejaculations. Amazing!

What is even perhaps more interesting, though, is that these were not the actual sins of Jerusalem. They were simply figures of speech, used by God to describe Israel's unfaithfulness to Him.

God was not satisfied with just drawing a parallel between Jerusalem's unfaithfulness and *"whoredom."* God Himself specifically chose to describe Jerusalem's spiritual *"whoredom"* in a very graphically sexual way.

Now, again, He could have stated just that they had been unfaithful to Him. Instead, He used very explicit language; a language with which Jerusalem evidently would have been very familiar – otherwise He would not have used it. "Hung like a horse" is the language that most of us could understand clearly as well.

If someone were to speak at a "church" or "Bible study," and they referred to something figuratively using the same sexual metaphors that God used here in Ezekiel, what would be the reaction?

Would it be called perverse and obscene? Would it be denounced as unholy and godless? Yet the bottom line is that it would be speaking just like the God of the Bible.

It would be safe to say that most people, who claim to be Christian, simply do not know the Bible or God very well. Jesus had similar problems. Many accused Him of being a sinner, a glutton, a drunkard, possessed of demons, and a servant of the devil.

The reason why more people haven't recognized such accounts as the one in Ezekiel is because they are reading a less than candid translation. Instead of translating the Bible exactly as they found it, they decided it needed a little "cleaning up." Yet it was God who made it "messy" to begin with. They seemed to have missed that. So we end up being left in the dark more often than we think. This makes the issue of studying all the more important.

5. *Strong's Hebrew Lexicon* #2231, *zirmah* (zir-maw'), feminine of 2230; a gushing of fluid (semen):-- issue.
6. *Wilson's Old Testament Word Studies.*

Chapter 21

JESUS AND THE COMMON MAN

The Lord Jesus Christ was the friend of the common, ordinary man.

*And the **common** people heard Him gladly* (Mark 12:37).

THE SANCTIMONIOUS SPIRIT
OF RELIGION

There was an elite religious movement during the earthly teaching ministry of Jesus Christ that had created a false standard and sense of moral self-righteousness. They were offended by, and rejected Christ's connection with the common man.

The Son of man came eating and drinking, and they say, "Behold a man gluttonous, and a winebibber, a friend of publicans and sinners." But wisdom is justified of her children (Matthew 11:19).

And when the scribes and Pharisees saw Him eat with publicans and sinners, they said unto His disciples, "How is it that He eats and drinks with publicans and sinners?" (Mark 2:16).

THE MEANING OF VULGAR

We hear a lot about things that are supposed to be "vulgar."

Now *there's* an interesting word. So much so, we've decided to use it as the title of this chapter.

Vulgar simply means "common." The Pharisees of Jesus's day would see Him with the common man and cry "common" (or "unclean"). They were calling them "vulgar." Commonness was viewed as "dirty" (or "unclean").

Noah Webster, in his 1828 dictionary, gives the etymology of the word *vulgar* as "the common people."[1] Thus, his corresponding definition of the word *vulgar* is as follows:

1. Pertaining to the common … people.
2. Used or practiced by common people.
3. Vernacular; national.
4. It might be more useful to the English reader, to write in our vulgar language.
5. Common; used by all classes of people; as the vulgar version of the Scriptures.
6. Public.

Of particular interest, notice the use of *"our vulgar language"* (4), and *"the vulgar version of the Scriptures"* (5).

EXAMPLE FROM THE TRANSLATING OF THE SCRIPTURE INTO THE VULGAR TONGUE

The word *vulgar* is used in the *"Translators to the Reader,"* the preface to the *King James Version*.

> Indeed without translation into the **vulgar** tongue, the unlearned are but like children at Jacob's well (which is deep) without a bucket or something to draw with; or as that person mentioned by Isaiah, to whom when a sealed book was delivered, with this motion, "Read this, I pray thee," he was fain to make this answer, *"I cannot, for it is sealed."*

---

1. Noah Webster, *An American Dictionary of the English Language*, 1828, F.A.C.E. facsimile reprint.

But we desire that the Scripture may speak like itself, as in the language of Canaan, that it may be understood even of the very **vulgar.**

A VULGAR BIBLE

Notice that the *King James Version* translators believed that the Bible should *"speak like itself."* By this they meant that the Bible was originally written, and should be translated "very vulgar."

So, the translators set out to have a **vulgar** translation of the Bible. Did they succeed? In some ways they did. We can see some attempts to translate the Bible into the "common" (or vulgar) language of the people. The result is that there are some things that are recorded in the Scriptures that even in our day could be considered "vulgar" by our "dirty" definition of the word!

We shall take a brief look at two words. The first is an example of a "vulgar" word in the *King James Version*. Then we will look at a word that the *King James Version* translators could not bear to translate.

Piss

Piss – now there is a good *King James Version* word. The phrase *"pisses against the wall"* is one that is not likely to be considered very "proper" by some, yet here it is, right there in the Bible (*c.f.* I Samuel 25:22, 34; I Kings 14:10; 16:11; 21:21; II Kings 9:8).

This "very common" phrase can be viewed by some as "vulgar" and therefore would not be very appropriate for some Christian's vocabulary. It's o.k. to be in our version of the Bible, but not in our daily conversation.

The phrase *"pisses against the wall"* is a figure of speech for "men." How amazingly "unchristian" to some this *King James Version* phrase is viewed!

"Kotex"

Many people who read Isaiah 64:6, or hear it often quoted by preachers, get an unclear picture of what God is using to illustrate man's state in Adam.

> *But we are all as an unclean thing, and all our righteousnesses are as **filthy rags;** and we all do fade as a leaf; and our iniquities, like the wind, have*

taken us away (Isaiah 64:6).

The Hebrew word for "filthy" is indeed a very interesting one. It is Strong's *Hebrew Lexicon #5708, ed,* from an unused root meaning **"to set a period"** (compare #5710, #5749); or **"the menstrual flux (as periodical)."**

Isaiah was writing about a "menstrual rag" in particular, not just a "filthy rag" in general. He was saying that in Adam all our righteous deeds are like sanitary pads!

How crude and vulgar such an illustration would seem to many a mind affected by Victorian morals! So much so, that here the *King James Version* translators did NOT allow the English Scriptures to *"speak like itself."* Such literal translation was not acceptable to the Anglican Bishops translating the *KJV*. Nevertheless such terminology was clearly acceptable for God and Isaiah.

THE PHARISEES OF OUR DAY

The Pharisees are alive and well. They can be identified, at least in part, by their reaction to "common," or so-called "vulgar" things!

Calvin's Geneva – The Origins of "Obscenity"

A point from the Protestant Reformation will serve well to make the point. Calvin's Geneva was a religious experiment in what ended up being, in many ways, a Pharisaic legalism.

One historian has revealed:

> Here we find the severing of sacred and secular and the origins of "obscenity." Certain words were proscribed, particularly those relating to fundamental activities of the body, and it was a logical development of this unnatural and artificially induced horror of anything associated, however remotely, with sexual or evacuatory activities, that led to the Victorian concealment of even the legs of their pianos.[2]

Words, in or of themselves, are not intrinsically "good" or "bad." In fact, even religiously viewed "good" words only become "bad" words because of their usage and intent.

2. Frank Bottomley, *Attitudes to the Body in Western Christendom*, Lepus Books, 1979, p. 146.

Take *"Jesus Christ"* for example. Are there two lovelier words to the believer? Yet these same two words can be used in ridicule. It is not the words themselves, being "good" or "bad," but the intent of the heart in their use. There are no intrinsically "bad" words.

By way of application, hear the words of grace and liberty from our apostle, Paul:

> *I know, and am persuaded by the Lord Jesus, that there is nothing unclean of itself: but to him who esteems any thing to be unclean, to him it is unclean* (Romans 14:14).

That which is unclean, is not unclean of itself. That is, there is nothing that is intrinsically unclean. It is only "unclean" based upon self-imposed standards (*"but to **him who esteems** any thing to be unclean, **to him** it is unclean"*).

BAD LANGUAGE

For the believer then, *"bad language"* is not defined by the actual words used, but by the intent of the words. Words that are not spoken to edify (*i.e.,* build up) are the real *"bad words"* or *"bad language."*

Thus, Paul's instruction:

> *Let no corrupt communication proceed out of your mouth, but that which is good to the use of edifying, that it may minister grace unto the hearers* (Ephesians 4:29).

Paul here speaks of the misuse of the believer's tongue. The *"corrupt communication"* that he speaks of is not to be found in a list of so-called "bad words." The Pharisees have missed the point.

Paul defines the *"corrupt communication"* in the verse. *"Corrupt communication"* is whatever is NOT *"good to the use of edifying,"* whatever does NOT *"minister grace unto the hearers."* That is the language that is *"corrupt"* and should not proceed out of our mouths.

The word "corrupt" used by Paul is the Greek word *sapros,* meaning "rotten, *i.e.,* worthless."[3] Our speech always is to be with grace (Colossians 4:6) – not what we say, but how we say it.

"Bad language" is language that tears down, insults, hurts, is boastful, proud, sarcastic, gossiping, complaining, judgmental, deceitful, rude, offensive, unkind and bitter.

The words of this kind of language are the true "curse" words; words that speak cursing instead of blessing. Curse words are often characteristic of Adam's descendants.

> *Whose mouth is full of cursing and bitterness* (Romans 3:14).

Believers need not be so concerned about the so-called "bad language" of the lost world around us. This so-called "bad language" is but a moral, religious smokescreen – a diversion from those things which are really important – godly edifying.

"Good" Words Gone "Bad"

As we saw earlier with *"Jesus Christ,"* words can be used in different ways, *"good"* or *"bad."* Even from generation to generation, words can generally move from one "column" to the other.

The word "gay" is a great example. Is it a "bad" word? Of course not. As we have already learned, words are not "good" or "bad" in and of themselves.

After all, the *King James Version* speaks of "gay clothing" (James 2:3), and with the *Flintstones* "You'll have a gay old time."

The "F" Word

Let's take a look at a *really* "bad" four letter word – maybe the "worst" of all.

We're talking about the infamous "f" word.

Here is a great example of a "good" word gone "bad." Why is it a "bad word" though? Is it bad because it is a four-letter word? "Lord" is a four-letter word. So is "love."

---

3. *Strong's Greek Lexicon #4550.*

Is it the way in which the letters are arranged that make it a "bad word"? If it was "fukc" would it be a "better" word? How about "cufk"? Exactly what is it about this word that makes it so "bad"?

Has anyone ever checked into it, to see?

A study of the roots and history (etymology) of our English word "fuck" will reveal that it has not always been viewed as a "bad" word. In fact, quite the opposite is true; it was a "good" word once.

Robert Hendrickson in his work *Word & Phrase Origins* writes:

> Originally a quite acceptable word, *fuck* was recorded in an English dictionary as early as John Florio's *A World of Words* (1598).

> From the Old German ficken/fucken, "to strike or penetrate" …

> Its first recorded use is in 1503.

> *Fuck* began to become more rare in print in the 18th Century when human experience began to be disguised behind a "veil of decency."

Notice that it was an 18th Century "veil of decency" that gave the word "fuck" over to "uncleanness." It is the same "veil of decency" that in the 1950s would not use the "bad" word "pregnant" either, or, that would have a man and his wife sleep in separate beds, or even in separate rooms.

It was the same "veil of decency" that would cause Noah Webster, when revising the *King James Version* in 1833, to "clean up" what he believed to be morally offensive language in the *KJV.*

We will close out this section with what Noah Webster said in the introduction to his revision. Don't neglect this; it is interesting, revealing reading.

> In no respect does the present version [*King James Version*] of the Scriptures require amendments, more than in the use of many words and phrases which cannot now be uttered, especially in promiscuous company, without *violence to decency*. In early stages of society, when men are *savage or half civilized*, such terms are not offensive: but in the present state of refinement, the utterance of many words and passages of our version [*King James Version*] is

not to be endured; and it is well known that some parents do not permit their children to read the Scriptures, without prescribing to them the chapters. To retain such *offensive language,* in the popular version [*King James Version*], is, in my view, injudicious, if not unjustifiable; for it gives occasion to unbelievers and to persons of levity, to cast contempt upon the sacred oracles, or call in question their inspiration; and this weapon is used with no inconsiderable effect.

Further, many words and phrases are *so offensive,* especially to females, as to create a reluctance in young persons to attend Bible classes and schools, in which they are required to read passages which cannot be repeated without a blush; and containing words which, on other occasions, a child could not utter without rebuke. The effect is, to divert the mind from the matter to the language of the Scriptures, and thus, in a degree, frustrate the purpose of giving instruction.

Purity of mind is a Christian virtue that ought to be carefully cherished; and *purity of language* is one of the guards which protect this virtue.

I have attempted to remove, in a good degree, this objection to the version. It was my wish to make some further alterations in this particular; but difficulties occurred which I could not well remove.

So go the religious attempts at the "purity of language."

Chapter 22

Religion's Increase of Sin

For you suffer, if a man brings you into bondage, if a man devours you, if a man takes of you, if a man exalts himself, if a man smites you on the face (II Corinthians 11:20).

Over the centuries, religion, to keep its hold on the masses, has made many more things "sinful" than really are. By doing so, religion keeps increasing the "need" of itself. In fact, if we have had religious influence pressed upon us in our lives, many things that we have known as "sin" may indeed not be so.

Wherefore if you are dead with Christ from the rudiments of the world, why, as though living in the world, are you subject to ordinances (touch not; taste not; handle not; which all are to perish with the using); after the commandments and doctrines of men? Which things have indeed a show of wisdom in will worship, and humility, and neglecting of the body; not in any honor to the satisfying of the flesh (Colossians 2:20-23).

Sin, in a biblical sense, is that which is an assault against God (*e.g.* worship of other gods, the exaltation of one's self or others equal to or above the place of God), or against one's fellow man (*i.e.*, that which is harmful or hurtful to others).

God is the sole governor of the universe. Sin is what God says it is … If we learn to think of something as "sin" apart from biblical revelation, then our understanding of "sin" is illegitimate. Social standards do not teach us about sin. Church dogma, church councils, church leaders or church creeds do not teach us about sin.[1]

---

1. Philo Thelos, *Divine Sex: Liberating Sex from Religious Tradition,* 2002, pp. 3-4.

Religion always seeks to make new lists of "sins." Religion keeps adding to the "sin catalog." How many things do we regard as "sin" that, in all actuality, are only the chains of religion? If something is said to be a "sin" long and hard enough, does that make it a sin? No. Only God can define sin.

> *I know, and am persuaded by the Lord Jesus, that there is nothing unclean of itself* (Romans 14:14).

> *All things are lawful for me, but all things are not expedient: all things are lawful for me, but all things edify not ... I will not be brought under the power of any* (I Corinthians 10:23; 6:12).

Oh! that you and I may be among those who possess that clearness of spiritual insight and audacity of faith's freedom that will enable us to be who and what God made us to be, without the binding chains of man's religion. Oh! for the audacity to believe God over men; the audacity to be free; and the audacity to live in that freedom honorably before God.

> *Stand fast therefore in the liberty wherewith Christ has made us free, and be not entangled again with the yoke of bondage* (Galatians 5:1).

Don't give up your freeman status in Christ for bondage in the so-called "sins" of the religious system.

Chapter 23

The Use of Our Liberty

All things are lawful for me, but all things are not expedient: all things are lawful for me, but all things edify not (I Corinthians 10:23).

Under grace we are free to apply the things that we learn, and walk in them, so long as we do not hurt, or become a stumbling block to others. This is the principle of love – because,

Love works no ill to his neighbor: therefore love is the fulfilling of the law (Romans 13:10).

Here enter the context and principles of Romans chapter 14, and the importance of a walk of *personal* faith and *clear* conscience. We are free to exercise our liberty in Christ insofar as it does not offend the weaker brother's conscience and thus destroy him. Here are some principles that we could use and apply in specific circumstances:

Scriptural Understanding

We should seek a scriptural understanding regarding any particular issue. The intent would be to provide clarity of conscience and a true act of personal faith, while in love allowing others to do the same, even though they may see things differently than we do.

Deliberate Actions

We should seek to gain clear understanding of our individual purposes and intents prior to any actions. Our individual actions should always be:

(1) In light of our personal consciences

Now the end of the commandment is love out of a pure heart, and of a good conscience, and of genuine faith … Holding faith, and a good conscience … (I Timothy 1:5, 19).

(2) In light of our genuine desires (as well as likes and dislikes)

For it is God Who works in you both to will and to do of His good pleasure (Philippians 2:13).

Our actions should be deliberate and with forethought. This is what the Christian life is intended to be – rather than a mindless spur-of-the-moment "going along" – so that any action can be done heartily as unto the Lord.

Genuine Honor and Respect

We should honor and respect one another and not *trespass* each other's personal faith and consciences.

These principles would allow us to reflect our walk in liberty as an act of worshipful faith *and* a walk in love.

OUR FREEDOM IS IN CHRIST, AND LOVE

Restrictions of the law are, under grace, fulfilled in one word: love. We are to love our neighbor as ourselves. Love will never hurt or defraud one's neighbor.

Owe no man any thing, but to love one another: for he who loves another has fulfilled the law. For this, "You shall not commit adultery, you shall not kill, you shall not steal, you shall not bear false witness, you shall not covet;" and if there is any other commandment, it is briefly comprehended in this saying, namely, "You shall love your neighbor as yourself." Love works no ill to his neighbor: therefore love is the fulfilling of the law (Romans 13:8-10).

For, brothers, you have been called to liberty; only use not liberty for an occasion to the flesh, but by love serve one another. For all the law is fulfilled in one word, even in this; "You shall love your neighbor as yourself" (Galatians 5:13-14).

As members of Christ's Body, we *are* neighbors.

... Speak every man truth with his neighbor: for we are members one of another (Ephesians 4:25).

Love is the fulfilling of the law. This is why, to the pure, all things are pure, and there is nothing unclean of itself. This is why love is eternally bound to grace. Grace is the absence of law, and there is no need for a law where love is genuinely present ... *"and the greatest of these is love."*

Unto the pure all things are pure ... (Titus 1:15).

I know, and am persuaded by the Lord Jesus, that there is nothing unclean of itself ... (Romans 14:14).

All things are lawful for me, but all things are not expedient: all things are lawful for me, but all things edify not (I Corinthians 10:23).

And now abides faith, hope, charity, these three; but the greatest of these is love (I Corinthians 13:13).

FREEDOM IS TO BE BASED IN FAITH AND GRACE

It is extremely important that we remember that freedom (as well as *all* other areas of our lives) is to be based in faith and grace! These indeed are the foundational principles set forth in Romans chapter 14.

Faith

There is the principle of personal faith. Our walk before the Lord is to be one based upon faith! This faith is to be *personal,* and without the dominion of men.

Whatever is not of faith is sin (Romans 14:23).

Let every man be fully persuaded in his own mind (Romans 14:5).

Do you have faith? Have it to yourself before God (Romans 14:22).

Not for that we have dominion over your faith, but are helpers of your joy: for by faith you stand (II Corinthians 1:24).

Our walk is to be one borne out of *personal* faith!

Grace

Then there is the principle of divine grace. God does not want us to judge each other regarding our *personal* faith. This is a real test of grace in our lives. It is easy to love and accept those who mirror our beliefs and practices – that takes little if any grace; but to love and accept a brother who has differing beliefs and practices requires a work of God's grace in our hearts. What it really takes is the willingness to give up our assumed dominion over the lives of others.

Wherefore receive one another, as Christ also received us to the glory of God (Romans 15:7).

Who are you who judges another man's servant? To his own master he stands or falls … (Romans 14:4).

But why do you judge your brother? Or why do you set aside your brother? For we shall all stand before the judgment seat of Christ (Romans 14:10).

God has called us to a life of grace, not law – a life that proceeds from the heart and love, not from externals. Do we by grace afford others the liberty to study the Bible for themselves? Do we permit them to come to their own position of *personal* faith before God? Do we allow them to walk in accordance with that faith to His glory as an act of worship? Do we let them live their lives heartily, as unto the Lord, and not unto men?

And whatsoever you do in word or deed, do all in the name of the Lord Jesus, giving thanks to God and the Father by Him … And whatsoever you do, do it heartily, as to the Lord, and not to men … (Colossians 3:17, 23).

Whether therefore you eat, or drink, or whatsoever you do, do all to the glory of God (I Corinthians 10:31).

Chapter 24

Due Benevolence

Let the husband render to the wife due benevolence: and likewise also the wife to the husband.

~ I Corinthians 7:3

Paul's marital instruction is very clear: the consummated husband/wife relationship is to function on the basis of a perpetual state of marriage (the uniting as *"one flesh"*).

MARITAL BENEVOLENCE

The covenant (promise) of marriage (physical union), among other things, binds the husband and wife to the act of *"benevolence."*

The word translated *"benevolence"* in the *King James Version* is *Strong's Greek Lexicon #2133, eunoia,* which is a euphemism for "conjugal duty," while the word translated *"due"* is #3784, *opheilo,* meaning "to owe … to be under obligation."

Thus the husband and wife are under a covenant of obligation to conjugal duty (sexual *responsibility*) to each other. The husband is responsible by the covenant of marriage to *"render unto the wife due benevolence."* The wife is also responsible by the same union covenant to render to her husband *"due benevolence."*

Let the husband render to the wife due benevolence: and likewise also the wife to the husband (I Corinthians 7:3).

They are both in the *bonds* of sexual unity: as the wife's body belongs to her husband, so the husband's body belongs to his wife.

> *The wife has not power of her own body, but the husband: and likewise also the husband has not power of his own body, but the wife* (I Corinthians 7:4).

MARITAL FRAUD

Because of this "conjugal duty," if the husband or wife denies sexual intimacy, they defraud the other.

> **Defraud not one another,** *except it is with consent for a time, that you may give yourselves to fasting and prayer; and come together again, that Satan tempts you not for your incontinency* (I Corinthians 7:5).

Noah Webster defines *"defraud"* as, "To deprive of right … to withhold wrongfully from another what is due to him."

Our English word *"defraud"* obviously comes from the root "fraud," which is defined by Webster as, "artifice by which the right or interest of another is injured." For this reason *"defraud"* (*Strong's Greek Lexicon #650, apostereo*) is also translated in James 5:4 of the *King James Version* as *"kept back by fraud."*

At the core of the marital covenant is the union of two as one. Central to this union is the sexual *bond* of coitus. This is the meaning of "marriage" – "the act of uniting." Unless prohibited by genuine physical limitations, anything less than consistent sexual union between a husband and wife is a defrauding of the marriage covenant (the promise of physical union).

Much *fraud* takes place in marriage relationships. Many "marriages" could be scripturally declared *fraudulent* – the couple being in a state of fault (*i.e.,* "an omission of that which ought to be done"). Their relationship is merely a pretense of "marriage;" an upscale room-mate arrangement, a social partner – but not a biblical marriage.

SOLE EXCEPTION

Outside of genuine physical limitations, there is only *one* scriptural exception for the suspension of regular sexual intercourse between a husband and wife. Consistent conjugal intimacy[1] is to be set aside only for the purpose of *"fasting and prayer."*

> *Defraud not one another, except it is with consent for a time, **that you may give yourselves to fasting and prayer;** and come together again, that Satan tempts you not for your incontinency* (I Corinthians 7:5).

Clearly stated, *"fasting and prayer"* is the **only** biblical purpose for not actively engaging in martial sexuality. *No* other reason is given.[2] The principle therefore is quite simple: no sex, no food; no intercourse, no eating. I would dare say that if many couples followed this scriptural principle they would already be dead from starvation!

FASTING AND PRAYER

This *fasting* is not for medical or health reasons, for it is coupled with *"prayer"* – *"fasting and prayer."* This is fasting associated with prayer. This type of scriptural fasting is a response to overwhelming grief, sorrow and heaviness – all an atmosphere of a burdened soul.

This example given to us by Paul is of a couple who is overwhelmed and overburdened of heart and soul to such an extent that there is a mutual loss of physical desire and drive. They are in mutual harmony – *"with consent."* They have agreed to devote themselves to working through their trials by giving their attentions to spiritual rather than physical matters. They will take the time that they usually spend in eating and intercourse and apply it to their struggles. This would be such a natural process for situations of extreme circumstances; but this unique time that they share together before the Lord is only to be *"for a time."* The expression of their sexual intimacy will be resumed at the same time as their dietary life is reinstated. There is a clear correlation between the need and pleasure of eating and that of sex.

---

1. There is no legalistic rule of frequency; an innate interval being established by the nature of the couple, and even then with degrees of ebb and flow.
2. Paul does not even validate the Mosaic Law's prohibition of sexual relations during the menstrual period. This ceremonial "uncleanness" has been done away by the death of the Lord Jesus Christ.

MUTUAL CONSENT

Defraud not one another, **except it is with consent** *for a time, that you may give yourselves to fasting and prayer; and come together again, that Satan tempts you not for your incontinency* (I Corinthians 7:5).

This abstinence for the purpose of *"fasting and prayer"* is to take place **only** by *mutual consent.* Both the husband and wife are to be in agreement to this purpose.

FOR A TIME

Defraud not one another, except it is with consent ***for a time,*** *that you may give yourselves to fasting and prayer; and come together again, that Satan tempts you not for your incontinency* (I Corinthians 7:5).

Not only is this *"fasting and prayer"* and sexual abstinence to be by reciprocal approval, it is also to be **only** for a limited, agreed-upon period of time – *"for a time."*

Even in the most extreme trials of agony, there comes a time to raise up from the sorrow and continue with life. This can be seen in the life of King David of whom, after his grieving process at the death of his young son, it is written,

Then David arose from the earth, and washed, and anointed himself, and changed his apparel ... and he ate (II Samuel 12:20).

COME TOGETHER AGAIN

Defraud not one another, except it is with consent for a time, that you may give yourselves to fasting and prayer; and **come together again,** *that Satan tempts you not for your incontinency* (I Corinthians 7:5).

At the end of the mutually agreed upon period of time dedicated to *"fasting and prayer,"* the couple are to *"come together again."* The word here translated *"come"* in the *King James Version* is *Strong's Greek Lexicon* #4905, *sunerchomai,* meaning "cohabit (conjugally)."

The word *"again,"* *Strong's Greek Lexicon* #3825, *palin,* is defined as "oscillatory repetition." Webster defines oscillatory as "moving backward and forward like a pendulum; swinging; as an oscillatory motion."[3]

This entire passage on the marital relationship is exceptionally plain: the consummated husband/wife union is to function on the basis of a continuous state of marriage (the uniting as *"one flesh"*).

Violating these principles places the believer in a state of rebellion to God's most basic marital foundation. Other than for this rare exception of *"fasting and prayer,"* there is no place for sexual abstinence in the life of the married believer. Operating "marriage" in such abstinence is a contradiction of terms; it is an oxymoron, denying the very biblical meaning of "marriage." Couples living in such a state of fraud are breaking their marriage covenant – they are marital covenant breakers.

Intimacy of sexual relationship is designed by God to be the great *bond* of joy between husband and wife. This is not just a physical issue, but a spiritual one as well. Its importance and value are to be protected at all lengths – *"that Satan tempt you not for your incontinency."*

---

3. Noah Webster, *American Dictionary of the English Language*, 1828.

Appendix 1

The Building of a Woman

One of the stories which have excited the ridicule of the critics of the Bible is the account of the creation of woman. If a rib was taken out of man to form a woman, why, we are asked, is not one still missing? Foolish as such an objection seems on the surface (for the loss of more important members of the body are not transmitted by generation) it challenges us to a look into the Scripture more carefully. It is difficult to see any particular reason why a rib should be chosen for this purpose. Was it really a rib, or may the word be understood of some other part of Adam's body?

The Hebrew word here rendered "rib," though it occurs over forty times, is nowhere else so translated. It is not the Hebrew equivalent of the Chaldee *galag* (Daniel 7:5), the only other word which may be rendered "rib."

Our translators have sometimes given it as *side* or *side chamber*, as well as *corner, board, plank, leaves* and *halting*. Many of these, it must be conceded, have some semblance to a rib.

The word is almost always used in connection with the temple or the tabernacle. A knowledge of the structure of these buildings will help us to discover its true meaning.

Ezekiel describes the millennial temple as having *side chambers* in the walls (Ezekiel 41:5-26). Their size, and how they increase in width as the walls of the building decreased, their number and how they were connected – all of these architectural details leave us in no doubt that the word here means a *cell,* or *vault,* an enclosed space.

When we transfer this meaning to the tabernacle structure, it seems to fail utterly; but this is because the tabernacle walls themselves are not correctly described.

Of the four Hebrew words translated *"board,"* one is used exclusively of the *"boards"* of the tabernacle, except a single occurrence where it is rendered *"benches"* (Ezekiel 27:6). It is not at all likely, however, that *benches* were made of ivory. Rather the *prow* of the ship was made of this precious substance. The word has the meaning of a taper, and the *"boards"* of the tabernacle were in shape like an inverted V. Every detail of measurement and design confirms this fact. The walls of the tabernacle were hollow.

Coming back to the Hebrew word *tzehlag,* which is here found to mean a *cell* or *vault,* we now have no difficulty in applying it to the "sides" of the tabernacle, for these enclosed a tapered vault. The bars which ran through from end to end were inside of this tapered vault, as well as the rings through which they passed.

These two examples are sufficient to establish the basic signification of the word. It is a *hollow cell.* There is no reason for calling it a rib, unless we slavishly follow the *Septuagint,* which is not consistent in its renderings.

Having arrived at the conclusion that it was not a rib but a cell of some kind, it behooves us to inquire from the Scriptures themselves what its nature was, and also to seek corroboration for our position in the facts found in our physical frames. We need not fear any disagreement between scriptural truth and physical fact: they must and do agree. If they do not, we are wrong. If they coincide in our interpretation of their testimony, we are probably in possession of the truth.

It is a notable fact which is usually overlooked that humanity was *created male and female* (Genesis 1:27). The sexes were combined in one individual. Adam was first formed, then Eve. There was an interval between the creation of the man and the building of the woman. *After* the creation of Adam God planted a garden eastward in Eden. He put the man in the garden to dress it and keep it. He commanded the man as to what he was and was not to eat, and He brought every animal of the field to Adam, who gave them their names.

Let us press the fact, which is repeated in the fifth chapter, that *"In the day that God created man ... male and female created He them ... and called their name Adam in the day when they were created."* It is evident that the Scriptures are true, in a much stricter sense than many suppose, that the woman was taken out of man.

Nothing new was *created* when the woman was built. The man permanently lost part of his structure which God removed when He created his help meet. In other words, the sexes were separated and Adam retained only masculine functions and Eve was built from the feminine. Do not the facts of the physical world perfectly confirm this interpretation? How could the removal of a rib change Adam from a hermaphrodite to the exclusively masculine structure of his descendants? Such a combination of the sexes is true today of most plants and some worms and mollusks.

It seems most reasonable, then, to believe, on the evidence of Scripture as well as nature, that woman was not a separate creation from man, but was built from that part of his original structure which he now lacks.

This is fraught with much beautiful material for reflection. Man, once complete in himself, is now but a part of his original self. The primal perfection can only be attained by the union of the two. They are in very deed one flesh. The One who severed them from one another in that deep sleep which fell upon Adam is the One who yokes them together in holy wedlock.

Is not this the key to our Lord's discourse against divorce? He is very emphatic. *"From the beginning of creation He makes them male and female."* This can refer only to the time when both were included in the one human being, Adam. Hence, *"On this account a man will be leaving his father and mother and will be joined to his wife, and the two will be for one flesh, so that they are no longer two, but one flesh. Then that which God yokes together let no man be severing."*

Here, indeed, we have the divine illustration of our union with Christ. Though it seems beyond belief, He is incomplete without us. We were chosen *in Him* before the disruption and now we become one with Him in redemption. Here there is no divorce possible. The ecclesia is His *complement* or fullness. It takes both to make a perfect Body for the Christ. The transcendent nature of this grace can be absorbed only by mature meditation. May we have grace to enjoy it fully!

A.E. Knoch
Unsearchable Riches, Vol. XI, No. 6
pp. 271-274, August, 1920

Postscript:

Concordant Version Note on Genesis 2:21

This stem is rendered "beam," "board," "chamber," "corner," "leaf," "plank" and "side" in the A.V. Only here is it *"rib."* It denotes an angular enclosed space. The *"boards"* of the tabernacle consisted of two planks, forming an angular vault. Here the female parts of humanity are severed from the male, to build the woman. The breasts of the male are a vestigial reminder that humanity was originally bisexual.

Sex Keeps You Healthier!

According to recent medical research, sex has been found to be a great healer as well as maintainer of a healthier life. Not only does regular sexual intercourse make women feel better emotionally, but it can give added health benefits – from glowing skin to your body fighting off diseases. These benefits include:

Sex Helps Regulate Your Hormones

Your endocrine system produces your body's hormones. Hormones stimulate orgasms and tissues in your body and cause them to perform in special ways. One of the hormones affected in women is estrogen. A woman who has sex regularly has been found to have higher levels of estrogen. What does this mean? Estrogen helps keep your circulatory and cardiovascular system functioning at a good level. It maintains the thickness in your bones or bone density. Estrogen helps keep skin smooth and more youthful. It helps ward off depression.

Sex Helps Regulate the Menstrual Cycle

Regular sexual intercourse can help regulate your menstrual cycle.

Orgasms Are Pain Killers

This truth shoots down the excuse of millions of wives who moan, "Not tonight, dear, I have a headache." Sex just might be your aspirin for that headache. It has been shown that when a woman has an orgasm, her body releases endorphins. Endorphins are released by the brain and act as a pain killer, like morphine.

Sex Can Help Ease Pre-Menstrual Syndrome (PMS)

One of the major symptoms of PMS is bloating and cramps. This is caused in part by the buildup of blood in the pelvic area five to seven days before your period. The muscle contractions produced during orgasm can help counter this by forcing the flow of blood out of this area and back into the main flow of your circulatory system.

Sex Is Better than "Nytol"

Sex can relieve stress and soothe and calm your body. It actually works as a sedative.

Sex Boosts Your Immune System

It is believed that after a woman experiences orgasm, her T-cell level increases. T-cells are white blood cells that help fight off foreign agents in the body and control the population of antibodies in our body's immune system.

Sex Is a Great Aerobic Workout

During sex, our heartbeat and pulse rate increase much as they do in an aerobic exercise. Now, I don't want to give you the impression that you burn as many calories in lovemaking as you do during a five-mile jog, but regular sex over a period of time can prove beneficial to your weight loss program.

Sex Helps Your Mental Alertness

Regular sex stimulates your nervous system, promotes mental alertness and heightens your five senses. It can make the whole world look rosier and brighter. Good sex can give you a high that no drug can equal.

So, wives, STOP looking at sex distastefully or as a duty! Good sex not only can make you feel better emotionally, it can make you look better physically and make you healthier. Regular, good sex with your husband can cut down your visits to the doctor!

Louis S. Greenup, Jr.
How to Stop the Other Woman from Stealing Your Husband, 1998, pp. 83-84.

Appendix 3

Health Benefits of Orgasm

We now know that even after menopause, it is important for a woman to have orgasms, not just because orgasms feel good, but also because orgasms are good for a woman's health. According to Dr. Alex Vermeulen, MD, Ph.D., professor of medicine, University of Ghent, Belgium, "Sexuality should be just as much a part of life after menopause as before."

Regular orgasms are also important for men. For example, it is an accepted medical fact that men with infected prostates can only overcome their condition with frequent ejaculations, along with antibiotics. According to some doctors, regular ejaculation is good preventative medicine, keeping the prostate well-drained.

In older single men, impotency can occur simply because he's been abstinent. The flaccid penis, which is probably the most oxygen-deprived organ in the body, needs oxygen to be healthy. If a man's blood vessels clog with cholesterol as he ages, there is less blood flow and even less oxygen. According to Irwin Goldstein, M.D., professor of urology at Boston University School of Medicine, abstinence can result in total erectile failure. "Bad things happen to tissues that are deprived of oxygen and the penis is no exception." (*Sex: A Man's Guide,* Emmaus, PA., Rodale Press, 1996, pp. 4-5).

Tom Gruber
What the Bible Really Says About Sex, 2001, Trafford Publishing, p. 69

Appendix 4

Marriage Is Good Medicine for Men

The biggest fiction behind James Bond is that the fantasy master spy and world-class heartbreaker lived past 40-something. It's not just the death traps and vodka martinis, or even the three packs of cigarettes a day that would have shortened his life. His naked ring finger would have too. Because real men need wives.

Consider the data: Married men – regardless of age, sex, race, income or education – consistently have been found to be healthier than men who are single, divorced or widowed. This so-called "marriage benefit" begins to kick in right after the wedding, then builds. Husbands ages 18 to 44 are strikingly healthier than bachelors of the same age. At every age, in fact, marriage not only protects men's health but also prolongs their lives. So, what's behind this marriage benefit?

Touch Therapy

It starts with the simple act of holding hands and hugging – long and loving embraces, several times a day, according to the latest science.

In the first study of how human touch affects the body's response to stress and threatening situations, Dr. James Coan, a psychologist in the departments of psychology and neuroscience at the University of Virginia, recruited married volunteers, slid them into MRI machines and warned them to expect an electric shock on their ankles. When spouses reached into the machines to hold their respective partner's hand – a simple yet loving gesture of support – the part of the brain that registers the anticipation of pain "turned off." The volunteers also said that they felt less distress.

The hand-holding also reduced agitation in the hypothalamus, the area of the brain that controls the release of stress hormones, which turn off our immune function. Eventually, a weakened immune system can make us sick.

"We can't see what our spouses are doing to our brains and emotions until a stressful event arises, but it's going on all the time," says Dr. Coan. "When a wife holds or caresses her husband, she is really reaching into the deepest parts of his brain, calming down the neural-threat response."

Can it be that easy access to a wifely hug after a fallout with a neighbor or a pounding on the golf course is as potent as a tranquilizer or a beta-blocker?

Men Need Nudging

Our proclivities are as old as Adam and Eve: Left to their own devices and vices, men are inattentive to physical symptoms. Even when they do notice, they try to deny them. Women are the health sentries. They pay careful attention to their husbands' well-being, pick up signals and symptoms, and get their men to the doctor. Put simply, most men depend exclusively on their wives to monitor, medicate, nurse and *nudge* them – in the here-and-now and through their waning years.

Having a partner helps men with cancer – specifically, cancer of the prostate or bladder – survive longer and with a better quality of life, according to studies at the Jonsson Comprehensive Cancer Center at UCLA. The same is true for men hospitalized with heart disease: In a study at the University of California at San Diego, coronary-bypass patients whose wives visited them early and often in the intensive-care unit required less pain medication and recovered more quickly than men without a spouse. Conversely, the patients whose wives did not provide much emotional support fared worse. Which leads us to a harsh reality: Not every marriage is good medicine.

Love Is the Key

Evidence is mounting dramatically that the quality of a marriage is strongly related to health. In fact, a man who has a secure marriage and who continues to be sexually active lives longer, succumbs to illness less often and heals from wounds and surgery faster. Why? It all comes down to insulating a spouse from chronic stress – regardless of whether the stress is physical illness or emotional distress, such as anger and anxiety.

The wiring circuits for emotion in the brain turn out to be sitting directly next to – and are deeply connected to – the circuits that control heart rate, blood pressure and how much adrenaline one secretes. "You can see the two circuits talking to each other on imaging machines," says Dr. Harry Lodge, an internist in New York City and co-author of *Younger Next Year.* "A bad emotional state makes needles jump. A really good marriage is harder to measure – it's an absence of those jumps."

If a couple is accustomed to fighting and blaming and retreating from each other under duress, the dynamics of the relationship can seriously compromise their bodies' ability to heal. In an experiment conducted by Drs. Janice Kiecolt-Glaser and Ronald Glaser at Ohio State University, long-married couples were given minor blister wounds, then asked to discuss a disagreement. Compared to the harmonious couples, the hostile couples took up to two days longer to heal.

Likewise, cardiologists report that if there is an undercurrent of hostility or resentment in a marriage or a suspicion of extramarital affairs – in short, marital discord – the whole cardiac recovery process slows down. Only secure and happy marriages reap the rewards of better health and longevity.

Sex Matters

When all is said and done, a solid marriage with regular and enthusiastic sex can be the best preventive medicine of all. In a woman, repeated affectionate hugs release the "bonding hormone" oxytocin and reduce blood pressure, which helps to protect her heart. No surprise: Men need more than snuggling. In men, the levels of oxytocin can and do surge up to five times above normal, but only immediately before he reaches orgasm. In a study at Queen's University in Belfast, the mortality of about 1,000 middle-aged men of comparable health was tracked over the course of a decade. The men who had sex three or more times a week had a 50% reduced risk of heart attack or stroke. And those who reported the most frequent orgasms had a death rate one-half that of the less sexually active men.

Presumably, the longer a man spends in a contented marital state, the greater the cumulative benefit: Studies show that long-married men live up to five years longer than their contemporaries.

In his practice at Columbia University Medical Center, Dr. Lodge says that he finds it easy to recognize people with truly good marriages: "They cuddle a lot and are deeply affectionate. There's a luminescence to them – a deep, calm, subtle glow."

A good marriage, then, gives men – as well as the women they love – good reason to stay alive.

RX for The Good Life

Don't go it alone! The stress of divorce and its aftermath have health consequences that may not show up for years, according to a 2005 study by researchers from the University of Chicago and Duke University.

The longer a man spends in a divorced or widowed state:

• the higher his likelihood of developing heart or lung disease or cancer.
• the greater his risk of high blood pressure, diabetes and stroke.
• the more difficulties he will have with mobility, such as walking or climbing stairs.

Gail Sheehy
Parade Magazine
June 18, 2006

Appendix 5

Ejaculations Maintain Healthy Prostate for Men

ex is Good for You!

When you consider the health benefits, it makes sense that smart men would opt for lots of sex. First, erections are good for the penis: each time you have an erection, you recharge the penis with tissue-nourishing oxygen through increased blood flow. This is what ultimately keeps you going longer and stronger. This is even more vital for older men who have fewer nighttime erections to provide the oxygen replenishing.

Second, many urologists consider three or four ejaculations a week good medicine for the prostate, since each ejaculation empties the prostate of built-up secretions (kind of like the way a sneeze clears the nose).

Throw in the psychological benefits you get from having orgasms and you've got an equation for sexual health. And it makes no difference whether you're having intercourse or masturbating – as far as your body's concerned, a climax is a climax (*Men's Confidential*).

Finally, although I know this one will be tough to face, try to ejaculate regularly. Because the prostate provides some of the fluid in semen, ejaculation may help keep it well-drained. You can consider that a prescription.

Dr. Ken Goldberg, M.D.
Prime Health and Fitness, Volume II, No. 4

Appendix 6

The Surprising History of Gynecology

As historian Rachel Maines describes in her exhaustively researched if decidedly offbeat work, *The Technology of Orgasm: "Hysteria," the Vibrator and Women's Sexual Satisfaction* (Johns Hopkins Press, 1999), the vibrator was developed to perfect and automate a function that doctors had long performed for their female patients: the relief of physical, emotional and sexual tension through external pelvic massage, culminating in orgasm.

The vibrator, she argues, made that job easy, quick and clean. With a vibrator in the office, a doctor could complete in seconds or minutes what had taken up to an hour through manual means. With a vibrator, a female patient suffering from any number of symptoms labeled "hysterical" or "neurasthenic" could be given relief – or at least be pleased enough to guarantee her habitual patronage.

"I'm sure the women felt much better afterwards, slept better, smiled more," said Dr. Maines. Besides, she added, hysteria, as it was traditionally defined, was an incurable, chronic disease. "The patient had to go to the doctor regularly," Dr. Maines said. "She didn't die. She was a cash cow."

Nowadays, it is hard to fathom doctors giving their patients what Dr. Maines calls regular "vulvular" massage, either manually or electromechanically. But the 1899 edition of the *Merck Manual*, a reference guide for physicians, lists massage as a treatment for hysteria (as well as sulfuric acid for nymphomania). And in a 1903 commentary on treatments for hysterical patients, Dr. Samuel Howard Monell wrote that "pelvic massage (in gynecology) has its brilliant advocates and they report wonderful results."

But he noted that many doctors had difficulty treating patients "with their own fingers," and hailed the vibrator as a godsend: "Special applicators (motor driven) give practical value and office convenience to what otherwise is impractical."

Small wonder that by the turn of the 20th century, about 20 years after Dr. Joseph Mortimer Granville patented the first electromechanical vibrator, there were at least two dozen models available to the medical profession ... [that a] big selling point for the devices was their particular usefulness in treating "female ailments" can be gleaned from catalog copy and medical textbooks at the time.

A text from 1883 called *Health For Women* recommended the new vibrators for treating "pelvic hyperemia," or congestion of the genitalia. Vibrators were also marketed directly to women, as home appliances. In fact, the vibrator was only the fifth household device to be electrified, after the sewing machine, fan, tea kettle and toaster, and preceding by about a decade the vacuum cleaner and electric iron – perhaps, Dr. Maines suggests, "reflecting consumer priorities."

Advertised in such respectable periodicals as *Needlecraft, Woman's Home Companion, Modern Priscilla* and the *Sears, Roebuck* catalog, vibrators were pitched as "aids that *every* woman appreciates," with the delicious promise that "all the pleasures of youth ... will throb within you." ... The vibrator remained a staple of the doctor's armamentarium and the proper wife's boudoir until the 1920s.

Natalie Angier
The New York Times
February 23, 1999

Related Quotations from
The History Channel's *Sex in the Twentieth Century*

Women were not free to express themselves sexually, even in marriage. Therefore a woman who did enjoy sex, there was something sort of mentally wrong with her. If a woman did suffer from an unfeminine desire to partake of the pleasures of the flesh, the physician often diagnosed her condition as a form of *hysteria*. – David J. Langum, author of *Crossing Over the Line*

They would get taken to the doctor's office and literally masturbated by hand, to have a *"relieving treatment"* (*i.e.,* an orgasm). And then they would send her home, and I suppose they told their husbands they needed another appointment as soon as possible.

Many people know that the advent of electrical appliances transformed the American home. But what a lot of people don't know is in the top five of those appliances, along with the electric iron and toaster, was the electric vibrator. – Susie Bright, author of *The Sexual State of the Union*

The vibrator first appeared in America as a tool in the doctor's office. There was a floor mounted vibrator called the Chattanooga, and this could produce the hysterical catharsis in a matter of minutes ... The woman would go home with a smile on her face, freed from her sexual fantasies, at least until next week when she would come back to the doctor.

Prior to the twentieth century this special treatment accounted for as much as three-fourths of some physician's practice, until technological refinements allowed women to apply the therapy in the privacy of their own homes. – Jim Peterson, author of *The Century of Sex*

Appendix 7

Joyful and Naked

A Joyful Noise

Most men want their wives to be naked and noisy. Most wives want to be covered and quiet. Wives, you must understand that men are made in the likeness of God, who likes for us to make a joyful noise unto Him (Psalm 98:4; 100:1).

Guess what? Husbands enjoy noise, too. Perhaps a *"joyful noise"* is the only sexual vocabulary that you will ever need to develop. Husbands love to hear sounds from their wives during sex. It lets them know that you are enjoying it as much as they are. There's no wrong sound during these times. From a moan to a compliment, it all sounds good to your husband.

Erotic sounds during lovemaking greatly increase a man's enjoyment of sex. Silent sex, to a man, is like a great meal without salt. The food was filling and satisfied your hunger, but it didn't excite your taste buds. Silent sex is filling in that it satisfies your husband's need for sex, but it isn't as exciting and exhilarating as noisy sex.

Naked and Open Before Him

There are women of all sizes, shapes and colors who have a problem being naked before their husbands. Wives, you shouldn't be ashamed to be naked before your husbands. Your physical imperfections mean nothing when you're a confident lover. In an article entitled *What Men Want To Tell Women About Sex but Don't*, the author says men find women with huge flaws attractive – if those women are confident and don't make a big deal about them. A sexy wife emphasizes the positive and shows enthusiasm about her relationship with her husband. She is alluring and not ashamed.

There's no need to be ashamed. Hebrews 4:13 says,

> *Neither is there any creature that is not manifest in His sight: but all things are naked and opened unto the eyes of Him with Whom we have to do.*

Genesis 1:31 says,

> *And God saw every thing that He had made, and, behold, it was very good. And the evening and the morning were the sixth day.*

In Genesis 2:25, you will find that Adam and Eve, before the fall, wore no clothes – they showed it all … Flaunt what God has blessed you with. You shouldn't be ashamed to reveal your naked body to your husband. Abishag in the Song of Solomon had no problem revealing her body to Solomon.

Solomon declared,

> *Thou art all fair, my love; there is no spot in thee* (Song of Solomon 4:7) …

So get undressed and give your husband an eye full!

Louis S. Greenup, Jr.
How To Stop the Other Woman from Stealing Your Husband, 1998, pp. 6, 56-57

Appendix 8

Song of Solomon

The Song of Solomon is the most straightforward sexual book in the Bible. Its theme is that of two lovers who take pure delight in each other's bodies and sexual love …

Nowhere in the Bible do we find a clearer illustration of God's attitude toward sex and the human body than in the Song of Solomon. Few people understand the graphically erotic nature of this love poem. Its explicit yet unashamed eroticism has been the cause of problems for commentators even before New Testament times. …

The issue of whether the book is to be interpreted literally or allegorically is irrelevant. That God used erotic language in either case says something about God that we must consider carefully. If the language God uses in this book is unfitting to be used in a literal sense, how can we possibly argue that it is good to use it in an allegorical sense? If the allegory is appropriate, then so is the language in which the allegory is framed. Sex and sexual language, in this case very explicit language, cannot be inherently nasty and still be used as an allegory. …

The language God uses here and the sexual situations He describes cannot be thought of in any other way than that God delights in and approves of what He is writing about. In doing so, God reveals more about His attitude toward sex, the naked human body, and the beauty and sexual eroticism involved in looking at another's sexual organs, than most church leaders and most Christians can handle …

God *designed* the male body and the female body *specifically and intentionally* to be sexually attractive to each other. There is such an openness in this book in describing the body and the act of love-making, and such a delight in the whole process that we humans surely should take thought about the legitimacy of our attitudes toward these things … If God sees all this as beautiful, clean, desirable and even holy, how can we view it as dirty and needing to be kept in the closet? … If God brings sex out of the closet for all the world to see, then we must resist every urge to stuff it back in there …

In the Song of Solomon we have one of history's best classical pieces of sexual literature. It represents erotic sex, desire and nudity in a straightforward, unashamed, even joyful setting. If the actual Hebrew words of that poem were translated into their modern language equivalent, this poem would surely stimulate sexual desire in some who read it.

Philo Thelos
Divine Sex: Liberating Sex from Religious Tradition, 2002, pp. 33, 81, 89, 90, 135

Appendix 9

Abstain from All Appearance of Evil
A Misunderstood Verse – A Freedom Robber!

*Y*ears ago in my first church Judy and I went to the movies. As we dropped off our then infant son at the home of one of the church members we were asked, "Where are you going tonight?" We replied happily, "To see a movie." At that point we knew we said something that we shouldn't have said. There was a disappointment on their face that their pastor was going to the movies. Later it was said that they don't go to movies because it has the *"appearance of evil."* In my life up to that point I had never had a problem with going to see a show but now I did – thanks to them!

What does the verse mean, *"Abstain from all appearance of evil"*? (I Thessalonians 5:22).

Since that dreadful movie day I've heard this verse quoted to prevent Christian freedoms more than any other verse. I've seen it quoted against simple things like beards on men ("you know that men who wear beards are evil"), to a woman's style of dress ("good Christian women do not wear pants to church, we are to avoid the appearance of evil").

I've come to see that this little verse has become one of two large buckets for condemning something or someone that the "legalist" doesn't like, the other being the "stumbling block" bucket! Both buckets are sweeping type statements that might be meant to help the fellow Christian but in actuality they squelch Christian freedom and ultimately evangelism. They are used when the legalist has not found a definitive biblical response. They then say something like, "God wants us to avoid all appearance of evil in our lives." So it is time we examine this misused verse to see if that is what God really is saying.

After our encounter with our church member who had a problem with us going to the movies, I was driven to examine the passage that was quoted. On the surface it looked very clear: *"Abstain from all appearance of evil"* (I Thessalonians 5:22). But as I looked at the context I realized that there was more to it than simply not doing something that someone might find questionable. At the time I had picked up a wonderful book by Joseph C. Aldrich entitled *Life-Style Evangelism*. In it he addressed this very verse in a chapter called "Avoid Evil Instead of Its Appearance." He says the following:

> In the Thessalonians passage quotes, Paul is talking about prophetic utterances in the previous verses (19-21). *"Do not put out the Spirit's fire; do not treat prophecies with contempt. Test everything. Hold on to the good. Avoid every kind of evil."* What is to be tested? The content of every prophetic utterance. What is good is to be held on to; what is evil is to be rejected. The passage is not saying never do something which looks like sin to another person. Jesus Christ frequently offended the leaders of the religious community.[1]

Aldrich pointed me in the direction of the context of the passage and to allow the context to dictate what the verse was saying. Let's see the verse in its context:

> *Quench not the Spirit. Despise not prophesyings. Prove all things; hold fast that which is good. Abstain from all appearance of evil* (I Thessalonians 5:19-22).

In the text the Apostle Paul is telling them to allow prophetic revelations of the Spirit, test the utterances, keep what is good and abstain from those that appear bad. It is that simple. Paul is not telling them to avoid actions that might look bad to someone else as many say today.

So what do other Biblical Scholars and commentaries say?

Here are a few.

---

1. Joseph C.Aldrich, *Lifestyle Evangelism: Crossing Traditional Boundaries to Reach the Unbelieving World,* Portland: Multnoma Press, 1981, p. 48.

William Hendriksen says, regarding verses 19-22,

> The reason for this disparagement of prophetical utterance can readily be surmised. Wherever God plants wheat, Satan sows his tares ... Paul, therefore, states what course of action the congregation should take: *"Prophetic utterances do not despise, but test all things."* ... Once a true verdict has been reached, the practical rule must apply: *"to the good hold on; from every form of evil hold off."*[2]

The Expositors Bible Commentary:

> From Paul's next prohibition, *"Do not treat prophecies with contempt,"* it appears that the Christians at Thessalonica like those at Corinth (I Corinthians 14:1) had underrated the gift of prophecy ... Apparently, however, certain "idle" brothers (:14; *c.f.* 4:11-12) had misused this gift by falsifying data regarding the Lord's return. This had soured the remainder of the flock against prophecy in general ... Paul stipulates that all ... manifestations be tested with a view to accepting what is valid and disallowing what is not (:21-22) ... Allowance must also be made for professed spiritual manifestations that do not contribute but rather detract from the development of the local body ... *"Hold fast"* to the good, but *"hold yourselves free from"* every kind of evil that tries to parade as a genuine representation of the Spirit.[3]

Hogg and Vine state:

> ... But if, on being tested, the tongue, prophesying or teaching, was not approved, the saints were to turn away therefrom.[4]

And lastly, New Testament Greek Scholar A.T. Robertson in summary says:

> Abstain from *every* form of evil ... Evil had a way of showing itself even in the spiritual gifts, including prophecy.[5]

---

2. William Hendriksen, *New Testament Commentary, 1 & 2 Thessalonians,* Grand Rapids: Baker Book House, 1975, pp. 140.
3. Robert L. Thomas, *Expositors Bible Commentary, Volume 11,* 1 Thessalonians, Grand Rapids: Zondervan Corporation, 1978, pp. 292-293.
4. C.F. Hogg, W.E., Vine, *The Epistles of Paul the Apostle to the Thessalonians,* Glasgow: Pickering & Inglis, 1914, pp. 200.
5. A.T. Robertson, *Word Pictures in the New Testament – Vol. 4,* The Epistles of Paul, Nashville: Broadman Press, 1931, p. 38.

So why have Christians misused this passage? I think it is their failure to get the context. I know it was mine! Yet once the context is read we can see what Paul was saying and it isn't that we avoid "questionable" behavior.

The problem with saying that Christians should avoid "questionable behavior" is that we have all kinds of opinions as to what is or is not questionable behavior. Obviously we are not talking about *sin* or wrongs as described and given by God. We most definitely are to avoid disobeying God. But when it comes down to matters of Christian freedom and liberty then this misapplication of I Thessalonians 5:22 must be challenged. I might not like what you do but if it isn't sin I should keep my mouth shut and allow you to enjoy your freedom in Christ. It is amusing to me, now that I've been a believer for over 30 years, how many things I've seen be "evil" to one generation of believers are not to the next. I can remember when guitars (even acoustic) were said to have the appearance of evil. Drums were not allowed in church, then they became allowed in Sunday night services and now they are found in the morning service of every growing church!

Were these things really evil? Not to God! The sad thing is that today's young Christians, who do things once taboo by the older generation, still find *"the appearance of evil"* in things that are pure and of no consequence to God.

So you might disagree with your fellow Christian who likes to dance, smoke cigars, has tattoos, enjoys a glass of wine or a beer for dinner, has piercings, or even drives a nice car (and "yes" I've heard this verse quoted in regards to the type of car one drives!), but you'll not find God saying in this verse to avoid such liberties because they have the appearance of evil. The verse isn't saying that!

Your actions and life choices are either *evil* or they are not. If what you do is evil then *don't* do it! If it isn't then you have the freedom to do it or not, it is up to you – even if others think it "looks bad!" You may be misunderstood by the legalists but you'll be in good company – Jesus looked bad to the religious people of His day.

> *Unto the pure all things are pure: but unto them that are defiled and unbelieving is nothing pure; but even their mind and conscience is defiled* (Titus 1:15).

Jeff Bowman
experiencegrace.com

Scripture Index

217

Bibliography

Aldrich, Joseph C., *Lifestyle Evangelism: Crossing Traditional Boundaries to Reach the Unbelieving World,* Portland: Multnoma Press, 1981.

Andersen, Uell, *Three Magic Words,* 1972.

Augustine, *The City of God.*

_____, *On Marriage and Concupiscence.*

Bailey, Derrick Sherwin, *The Mystery of Love and Marriage.*

Barclay, William, *Daily Celebration.*

Biale, David, *Eros and the Jews,* 1993.

Bloch, Iwan, *The Sexual Life of Our Time: In Its Relations to Modern Civilization,* Allied Book Company, n.d.

Bottomley, Frank Attitudes To The Body In Western Christendom, Lepus Books, 1979.

Bright, Susie, *The Sexual State of the Union.*

Bulwer, *History of Athens.*

Cairncross, John, *After Polygamy Was Made A Sin: The Social History of Christian Polygamy,* London: Rouledge & Kegan Paul1974.

Campbell, James, *A History and Philosophy of Marriage,* Patriarch Publishing House, 2007.

Carr, David M., *The Erotic Word,* Oxford University Press, 2003.

Cole, William Graham, *Sex in Christianity and Psychoanalysis,* Oxford University Press, 1955.

Dawson, P.R., *Marriage: A Taste of Heaven,* Gospel Themes Press, 1995.

Ecker, Ronald L., *And Adam Knew Eve.*

Epstein, L.M., Sex Laws and Customs in Judaism, New York: KTAV Publishing, 1967.

Fausto-Sterling, Ann, *Sexing the Body: Gender Politics and the Construction of Sexuality,* 2000, New York: Basic Books.

Feldman, David M., *Marital Relations,* Schocken Books.

Friedman, David M., *A Mind of Its Own,* New York: Penguin, 2003.

Fulton, Justin D., *Why Priests Should Wed,* Evangelist L.J. King, Toledo, Ohio, 1913.

Gardelia, Peter, *Innocent Ecstasy,* Oxford University Press, 1985.

Gingrich, Roy, *The History of the Church,* Riverside Press, 1980.

Goldstein, Irwin, M.D., *Sex: A Man's Guide,* Emmaus, PA., Rodale Press, 1996.

Greenup, Jr., Louis S., *How To Stop the Other Woman from Stealing Your Husband,* 1998.

Gruber, Tom, *What the Bible Really Says About Sex,* Trafford Publishing, 2001.

Hendriksen, William, *New Testament Commentary, 1 & 2 Thessalonians,* Grand Rapids: Baker Book House, 1975.

Hillman, Eugene, *Polygamy Reconsidered,* Orbis Books, 1975.

Hitchens, Robert, *Multiple Marriage: A Study of Polygamy in Light of the Bible,* Elkton, MD, Doulos, 1987.

Hogg and Vine, *The Epistles of Paul the Apostle to the Thessalonians,* Glasgow: Pickering & Inglis, 1914.

Hornsby, T.J., *Sex Texts from the Bible.*

James, E.O., *Marriage Customs Through the Ages,* Collier Books, 1965.

Jerome, *Select Letters,* Loeb, 1966.

Jonas, Coelius, et al., *The Last Days of Luther,* translated and annotated by Martin Ebon, New York: Doubleday, 1970.

Jordan, James, *Judges: God's War Against Humanism.*

Kelsey, Morton and Barbara, *Sacrament of Sexuality: The Spirituality and Psychology of Sex,* Amity House, 1986.

Knight, III, George W., *Commentary on the Pastoral Epistles,* Grand Rapids, MI, W.B. Eerdmans Publishing Company, 1992.

Knoch, A.E., *The Building of Woman,* Unsearchable Riches, Vol. XI, No. 6, 1920.

Kraut, Ogden, *Pioneer Publishing,* 1983.

Królewiec, Stanislaw, *Christian Concubines,* (internet article).

Langum, David J., *Crossing Over the Line.*

Lawrence, Jr., Raymond J., *The Poisoning of Eros: Sexual Values in Conflict,* Augustine Moore Press, 1989.

Lazareth, William H., *Luther and the Christian Home,* Philadelphia: Muhlenberg Press.

Lehmann, Paul, *The Decalogue and the Parameters of a Human Future,* Association of Clinical Pastoral Education Conference, 1981.

Lewinsohn, Richard, *A History of Sexual Customs,* translated by Alexander Mayce, Harper & Brothers, 1958.

Lewis, C.S., *The Humanitarian Theory of Punishment,* June 1953.

_____, *Mere Christianity,* Book III, Christian Behavior.

Mace, David R., *The Sacred Fire,* Abingdon Press, 1986.

Maines, Rachel, *The Technology of Orgasm: "Hysteria," the Vibrator and Women's Sexual Satisfaction,* Johns Hopkins Press, 1999.

Marius, Richard, *Luther,* Lippincott, 1974.

McQuilkin, Robertson, *An Introduction To Biblical Ethics,* Tyndale House Publishers, 1989.

Noonan, Jr., John T., *Contraception: A History of Its Treatment by Catholic Theologians and Canonists,* Cambridge: Harvard University Press, 1965.

Patrick, John, *The Teahouse of the August Moon,* adapted from the novel by Vern Sneider, Dramatists Play Services, 1957.

Paulk, Earl, *Sex Is God's Idea,* K Dimension Publishers, Atlanta, GA, 1985.

Peterson, Jim, *The Century of Sex.*

Robertson, A.T., *Word Pictures in the New Testament – Vol. 4,* The Epistles of Paul, Nashville: Broadman Press, 1931.

Scanzoni, Letha, *See No Evil, The Other Side,* 1978.

_____, *Sex and the Single Eye,* Zondervan, 1968.

Shakespeare, William, *Venus and Adonis*

Sheldrake, Philip, *Befriending Our Desires: Unity of Agape and Eros,* 1994.

Shipley, Tom, *Man and Woman in Biblical Law: A Patriarchal Manifesto (They Shall Be One Flesh, Part II),* 2009.

Spong, John Shelby, *Living in Sin,* Harper, San Francisco, 1988.

Stace, Robert W., *Why Weren't We Told?* 2001.

Tannahill, Reay, *Sex in History,* Scarbough House, 1992.

Taylor, G. Rattray, *Sex in History: The Story of Society's Changing Attitudes to Sex Throughout the Ages.* The Vanguard Press, Inc., New York, 1970, page 164.

Thelos, Philo, *Divine Sex: Liberating Sex from Religious Tradition,* 2002.

Thomas, Gordon, *Desire and Denial,* Brown and Little, 1986.

Thomas, Robert L., *Expositors Bible Commentary, Volume 11,* 1 Thessalonians, Grand Rapids: Zondervan Corporation, 1978.

Tillich, Paul, *Love, Power and Justice,* 1954.

Todd, John M., *Luther,* New York: Crossroad, 1982.

Troeltsch, Ernst, *The Social Teachings of the Christian Churches,* II, trans. Olive Wyon, Allen & Unwin, 1931.

Wall, Otto A., *Sex and Sexual Worship,* College Park, MD., McGrath Publishing, 1970.

Ward, Roy Bowen, "Women in Roman Baths," *Harvard Theological Review.*

Wilhelm, Charles J., *Biblical Dyslexia,* 2004.

Woodrow, Ralph, *Women's Adornment.*

Standard Reference Works

A New Standard Bible Dictionary, Funk & Wagnalls, 1926.

An American Dictionary of the English Language, Noah Webster, 1828.

American Heritage Dictionary.

An Etymological Dictionary of Modern English, Ernest Weekly.

Anthon's Classical Dictionary.

Baker's Evangelical Dictionary of Biblical Theology.

The Barnhart Concise Dictionary of Etymology, Robert K. Barnhart.

Cambridge Dictionary.

The Concise Dictionary of English Etymology, Walter W. Skeat.

The Exhaustive Concordance of the Bible, James Strong, Nashville: Abingdon, 1981.

Dictionary of Word Origins, Joseph T. Shipley.

Dictionary of Word Origins, John Ayto.

Eerdman's Bible Dictionary.

Eerdmans' New Bible Dictionary, Editor J.D. Douglas; W.B. Eerdmans Publishing.

Funk & Wagnalls New Encyclopedia, 1986, Funk & Wagnalls.

A Greek-English Lexicon of the New Testament, Joseph H. Thayer, Grand Rapids, MI, Baker, 1995.

Halley's Bible Handbook, Henry H. Halley, Zondervan.

Harper's Bible Commentary.

Luther's Works, Vol. 54, p 177; Theodore G. Tappert & Helmut T. Lahmann eds., Philadelphia: Fortress Press, 1967.

Oxford Concise Dictionary, Oxford University Press.

Oxford Concise Dictionary of English Etymology, T.F. Hoad.

Origins: A Short Etymological Dictionary of Modern English, Eric Partridge.

Unger's Bible Dictionary, Moody Press.

Wikipedia Encyclopedia.

Wilson's Old Testament Word Studies.

Word & Phrase Origins, Robert Hendrickson.

A World of Words, John Florio, 1598.

Young's Analytical Concordance to the Bible.

ABOUT THE AUTHOR

Clyde L. Pilkington, Jr., has been teaching the Word of God for over thirty years. His life has been dedicated to the recovery and sharing of Biblical truths.

He pastored for 15 years (Hampton, VA), was a Christian school administrator, Bible bookstore owner (Amherst, VA), and active Bible conference speaker.

Other than family, literature has been the drive of his life. For the past twenty-five years this has found its expression in the distribution of serious, hard-to-find Bible study books, through a family-based ministry known today as **StudyShelf.com**™.

He has been the editor of *The Biblical Standard* (1976-1980), *The Old Paths* (1981-1985), *Forgotten Truths* (1986-1989), *Grace Testimony* (1986-1995), and currently the weekly *Bible Student's Notebook*™ (1989-present).

Clyde now resides in Windber, PA, enjoying the greatest roles of his life as husband, son, father and grandfather.

Your Part

Now that you have read this book, it's your turn.

If the truths presented here have helped you, don't let these truths die in your hands.

Please write to us and let us know your thoughts concerning its content.

Consider assisting us in getting this book into the hands of those who would be encouraged and strengthened by its message:

- Recommend it to your friends and loved ones.
- Order additional copies to give as gifts.
- Keep extra copies on hand to loan to others.

If you have not read the author's other works, order them today.

We would be honored to have your fellowship in getting this book freely to those who hunger spiritually. We have daily opportunities to send it to pastors, Sunday school teachers, Bible college professors and students, Bible class teachers, and prisoners.

DAILY E-MAIL GOODIES™

Do you receive our
Daily E-mail Goodies™?

These are free daily e-mails that contain short quotes, articles, and studies on biblical themes.

These are the original writings of Clyde L. Pilkington, Jr., as well as gleanings from other authors.

Here is what our readers are saying:

"Profound! Comforting! Calming! Wonderful!" – **NC**

*"I am glad to be getting the **Daily E-mail Goodies** – keep 'em coming."* – **IN**

*"The **Daily E-mail Goodies** continue to bless my heart! … They provide plenty of food for thought."* – **IL**

*"I really appreciate the **Goodies!**"* – **VA**

*"Your **Daily E-mail Goodies** are making me aware of authors whose names I don't even know."* – **GA**

Request to be added to our free
Daily E-mail Goodies™

If you would like to be added to the mailing list, e-mail us at:

Goodies@StudyShelf.com

Do You Subscribe
to the

Bible

Student's

Notebook™?

This is a periodical that …

- Promotes the study of the Bible
- Encourages the growth of the believer in grace
- Supports the role of the family patriarch
- Is dedicated to the recovery of truth that has too long been hidden under the veils of traditionalism, prejudice, misunderstanding and fear
- Is not connected with any "Movement," "Organization," "Mission," or separate body of believers, but is sent forth to and for all saints.

The *Bible Student's Notebook*™ is published weekly (52 times a year).

Subscribe Today!

Your source for rare and hard-to-find Bible study materials for the serious-minded, hungry-hearted students of Scripture.

Over the years we have been often asked to recommend books. The requests come from believers who longed for material with substance. Study Shelf™ is a collection of books which are, in our opinion, the very best in print. Many of these books are "unknown" to the members of the Body of Christ at large, and most are not available at your local "Christian" bookstore.

Some of Our Authors	*Some of Our Topics*
Sir Robert Anderson	Alcohol
T. Austin-Sparks	Baptism
Charles F. Baker	Church History
E.W. Bullinger	Commentaries
H.A. Ironside	Dispensational
A.E. Knoch	Exchanged Life
Clarence Larkin	Gap Theory
C.H. Mackintosh	Government
William R. Newell	Home
J.C. O'Hair	Racism
C.R. Stam	Reference
Miles Stanford	Spiritual Growth
Charles Welch	Universal Reconciliation
Martin Zender	War

PILKINGTON & SONS
PO Box 265 Windber, PA 15963
www.studyshelf.com
1-800-784-6010

UPCOMING BOOKS
by Clyde L. Pilkington, Jr.

I Am! … Who God Says I Am
The Divine Reckoning
of the Renewed Mind

He Is!
What the Bible Says God is to Me

Reigning in Life
The Believer's Liberated Life in
Christ
(The Relationship of Identification
Truth to the Details of Life)

The Kingdoms of This World
A Biblical Look at Human
Government and the Believer's
Relationship to It

Racing Through the Bible
A Biblical Study of Ethnic
Divisions

Believer's Body Life
The Divine Viewpoint in our
Relationships

Night Lights
The Last Words of Dying Saints

God's Present Purpose
The Dispensation of the Grace of
God
(A Collection of Studies on Right
Division)

Every Day Alike
The Observance of Days in the
Age of Grace

God is Divorced Too!
Biblical Words of Comfort for the
Divorced

Select Readings
A Treasury of Gleanings

Bible Student's Treasury
A Collection of Articles from the
Bible Student's Notebook™

BIBLE STUDENT'S PRESS™
PO Box 265 WINDBER, PA 15963
WWW.BIBLESTUDENTSPRESS.COM
1-800-784-6010

CPSIA information can be obtained
at www.ICGtesting.com
Printed in the USA
BVOW10s0203100616

451336BV00003B/44/P